10-9
In The Fifth

Brenda Westrup

A CIP catalogue record for this book is available from the British Library.

Printed and bound in Great Britain.

ISBN 1 84024041 5

Prospero Books
46 West Street
Chichester
West Sussex
PO19 1RP

Cover designed by Sarah Williams

Many, many thanks to all the wonderful friends who supported us throughout all of Mike's illness and recovery period and who then went on to help me to produce this book.

Without their help there might not have been a happy ending and therefore no story to write.

To Mike - with love

Chapter 1

THE CHAMPION

Squash is a game played in a room. Two people hit a small black rubber ball against the wall and run around frenetically trying to retrieve it. It requires an inordinate amount of fitness, racket skills and, in order to succeed, some inborn natural talent; this enables you to judge where the ball is going and where to hit it in return. Some people liken it to a very energetic game of chess.

I discovered this crazy pastime at the age of thirty-something. Great fun! I could hit the thing and chase after it, but natural talent had I none. I had to make up for this deficit with enthusiasm.

My children were growing up and needing me less and less and I needed a leisure pursuit at the end of my working day as a physiotherapist. I eventually plucked up the courage to join a squash club. I had never belonged to any kind of club since being a Girl Guide, and it was a whole new world.

Every club has its personalities and Mike was one of them. Everyone loved Mike. He played for and captained the first team which he had led to victory in many prestigious events. I often watched him play. He was known for his good humour on court; he would grin amiably at his opponent and play the knock-up looking infinitely more like a rugby player than a squash player. Then, when the match began, he would usually win with good-humoured ease and frequent jovial remarks. His squash kit never matched, and this in the days when everyone had perfectly laundered and matching kit emblazoned with designer logos. There was Mike: odd socks, crumpled shirt and a pair of shorts with the seams looking worryingly as if one lunge at the ball and all might be revealed! I remember him winning a tournament on one particular occasion and being presented with a cash prize. The organiser jokingly remarked that he could now go out and buy himself some new kit. He looked so hurt. Who was looking after him? Who was failing to mend his shorts or launder his kit? Was he married? No-one knew. He was so much loved by everyone and yet so private.

In my little way I progressed to the second rung of the ladder and started to play team squash; I even became Ladies Captain, rather by default. My children were now at boarding school and life at home was such that I spent more time at the squash club. The top players were so much in a class of their own that one would never actually get to know them very well, but we all watched them play and cheered them on.

I was watching Mike play one day when he injured his ankle. Far be it for me to interfere and go down to offer my services, someone else did that, and he was then introduced to me. This was the first time I had actually spoken to him. He asked if I could give him some treatment and I said that I would.

The person who introduced us was to change our lives completely. I have a kind of belief in a 'Grand Plan', 'Divine Intervention', call it what you will, and I believe someone 'Up There' knew that, in the not too distant future, Mike was going to need a lot of loving and care from someone with some medical background and that I had a lot of love to give and probably fitted the bill. Neither of us had any

8

plans to form a relationship, we were not looking for it, and consequently it took a very long time to happen, and when it did it was very, very slowly.

There was I, a middle aged mother of two teenage sons, feeling extremely surprised and even rather ashamed of how I felt about this squash playing patient of mine. Professionalism dictated that I kept it very much to myself. Mike told me later that I did this most successfully; I appeared to be the cold, detached professional. Despite this, something made him come around to see me one lunch time; I was out so he left a note.

He then offered to give me a squash lesson and as this was now away from my professional role as a physiotherapist I willingly allowed the friendship to blossom. Four years, and a lot of emotional heart searching and traumas later I left my 'old life' and moved in with my friend, Sue. Six months, and even more emotional agony later, Mike and I bought a house together and my 'new life' began.

One thing often puzzled me. I kept on imagining Mike being very ill and in hospital, how I would cope, how I would nurse him myself and how I would explain this to the nursing staff. It was like a waking dream, it kept recurring and I dismissed it as fantasy. Mike at this stage had won the British Open Over 45 Tournament so was almost, by definition, the fittest over 45 year old in the country; how utterly absurd to be having thoughts like these.

We had a wonderful life, with Mike playing and often winning tournaments in this country and abroad. We had trips to Scotland, Ireland and Wales with him as the England Veteran Captain. He seemed untouchable by players of his age. He had a very individual style of play; he would bounce, taking a stride jump in the middle of the court which enabled him to set off quickly in whatever direction he needed; he also had a little angled shot off the side wall, called a 'boast', which no-one could ever see coming and which therefore caught everyone unawares. It was most unorthodox and I once heard someone say that Mike Westrup was the only person who could play squash badly well!

One year the team from Scotland, knowing that none of them stood a chance against Mike, decided to see who could stay on court the longest against him, so they produced a stop watch, which made it a very entertaining match.

In the January of 1992 it was the time for the National Championships, they were to be held in Cheadle, Cheshire, over a weekend. There is also another tournament called the National Challenge which goes on all year and the finals of that were to be held on the same weekend. Mike had made it through to the finals of the Challenge and was to play Alan Purnell from Birmingham. It was a lovely weekend with time in between the matches to explore the area. Mike had made it through to the finals of the main event by the Saturday morning and amazingly had to play the same person - Alan! They discussed how to arrange the match, one suggestion was to play one match for two trophies; Mike thought this was a dreadful idea so it was agreed that one match, the least important Challenge, would be played on Saturday afternoon and the main event on the Sunday morning. The Squash Rackets Association agreed although it did mean that the Sunday match would have to be rather early and would, therefore, not have many spectators, which was a pity.

Mike always found Alan very difficult to play, Alan being a left handed player with a lot of very good 'tennis' shots albeit on the squash court. Mike is known for his side wall shots, 'the boast', and Alan saw them all coming but I did notice that if Mike played the ball hard down the side wall he tended to win the point. This was not enough and in next to no time Mike was off court having lost. He had lacked all his usual bounce and sparkle and Alan had made the most of this. Never mind! It is only a game and he could have another 'go' tomorrow.

The next morning Mike woke with a headache which was most unusual. I gave him the only headache remedy I had with us and he had an early breakfast and then used me as a 'warm-up' opponent. This involved my going on court with him and hitting the ball to him. He would then usually play a winner which I would fail to return, so I would pick up the ball and start again. This was always pretty bad for my ego, but he found it very useful. People often wonder why my game is the way it is. I have gradually learnt to play winners off brilliant shots (I've had plenty of practise). There would be no point in my keeping the rally going because the next return from Mike was always destined for the 'nick' which is unreturnable. I have, therefore, become reasonably good against a skilled stroke player but hopeless against the lesser player who just whacks the ball.

Anyway, it was the usual format on this Sunday morning and Mike gradually started to feel a bit better. I then suggested that he changed his style of game and just hit the ball down the side wall - the element of surprise.

Poor Alan, not only was he playing a bouncy, sparkly Mike but also a Mike who was playing a totally different type of game. The spectator's gallery started to fill up and apparently those who watched the match said it was the best one that weekend. Mike won relatively easily, it was a mirror image of the previous night and this meant he had won the Over 45 National Championship for the third time. Realistically, it gets harder every year as younger competitors enter, so it is more of an achievement by the third year.

I have often wondered since, in the light of what I know now, whether the tablets I gave Mike for his headache did more than just relieve the pain, because he was such a different person on the Sunday. It was about the last time I was to see his brilliance on court.

Life was very sweet but then little things started to happen - I see them now with the benefit of hindsight. Mike started to gain weight, nothing dreadful, and everyone put it down to contentment. In April 1992 he entered the British Open Over 45 event again, not necessarily expecting to win because he was now a year older and there was young blood coming in. His first round match should have been no problem at all but he felt unwell, was unable to see the ball in the air and had a headache similar to a migraine although he had never had a migraine in his life. He had to scratch from the tournament, something he had never, ever done before. He was due to go on and play somewhere else later that evening, but he willingly let me cancel that and came straight home; this was not typical of my Mike.

In June my elder son, Nick, had his Graduation Ceremony at Cambridge and by that time Mike's suits were becoming tighter and tighter, but he struggled into one and off we went. It was a very hot day and I felt very proud of my son. My ex-husband was there with his Mother and it could have been an awkward mix of people but for the fact that talking has never been something that presented my ex mother-in-law with any problems and this actually eased the tension for everyone. Mike chatted away to her, but I realised that he had asked her the same question three times; I gently pointed this out to him, but he looked bemused.

The next event in our calendar was my Mother's 80th birthday. We arranged to take her and her old school friend of the same age, together with my two sons, Nick and Chris, and Mike's daughter, Karen, and her boyfriend to a hotel in Bournemouth.

It was a successful weekend but for the fact that Mike needed a sleep on the Saturday afternoon and was ready for bed by ten o'clock that evening. The two elderly ladies seemed to have more energy and it was all rather embarrassing. I made various excuses for Mike, about him having been working too hard recently and I sort of believed them myself, but not entirely.

We had arranged a holiday in September; we were to take the car to Corsica. Mike was definitely a little forgetful by this time, so I decided that a holiday was just what he needed. It was a long drive down to Nice where we were to catch the ferry to Corsica, and Mike did most of the driving with just the odd two hour break. He did so well that I wondered what I had been worrying about. The weather on the journey was dreadful and we had to really rush the last part of the journey and arrived only just in time. Any driver would have been tired by then but Mike seemed fine. We spent three nights at the first hotel. The only problem was that we had to leave our room key in a cubby hole and Mike could never remember the number. He also tended not to feel all that good in the mornings but would perk up at about eleven o'clock after a couple of coffees. The red Corsican wine is a bit rough so we thought that must be have been the cause, so we changed from a full bottle of red wine to a half bottle of rosé at dinner. This seemed to solve the problem. There was a tennis court and we played every evening before dinner. I never won a set, but it was fun trying!

The roads in Corsica are very beautiful if a little tortuous, often with horrendously steep drops to one side. You would find flowers on the roadside in memory of the person who last failed to negotiate the bend. I decided that Mike was definitely the better driver and I would map-read and close my eyes on occasions; he coped superbly. We found some idyllic beaches and I taught Mike how to snorkel. It was a whole new world to him and he was just starting to admit that he was enjoying it when I pointed out a small, minute in fact, jelly fish . The result was like a tidal wave and Mike plus flippers tried to leave the sea in one quick movement, and that was that. "If there are things like that in the sea then I do not wish to be there".

Our wonderful holiday came to end and we started the long journey home. It was the end of September.

Mike's daughter, Karen, had arranged for us to go the theatre together shortly after we came home. I was starting to feel uneasy about Mike driving to London, which seemed unreasonable bearing in mind how well he had coped on holiday. He seemed a bit dazed but managed. It was six months later, and many traumatic events on, that I mentioned to Mike about the show. He had absolutely no recollection of ever having been.

Chapter 2

OCTOBER

By October he was very tired in the evenings and still gaining weight. I was starting to worry. A doctor friend of mine, Jill, came to dinner and he was fast asleep by eight o'clock. I had voiced my fears to her during the day and I thought she might come up with some explanation. She went home that evening most concerned and after agonising over it for a couple of days she decided to ring me and suggest that I take Mike to the doctor for some pituitary and thyroid tests.

I was so glad that our doctor was also a friend of ours as otherwise I would have felt very silly taking Mike along. He looked so well, had no idea what all the fuss was about and the only real reasons that I could give the doctor for us being there was that Mike's squash had deteriorated, he had gained weight, was a bit sleepy in the evenings and had become slightly forgetful - all things that could be explained by the normal ageing process, only I knew that was not the case.

The simple blood test was done and we had to wait for the results. It was the weekend of the County Championships. This was an event where Mike's name featured more on the record sheets than anyone else. For years and years he had won the full championship and more recently he had often won the Over 35 event and was certainly very likely to win the Over 45.

We arrived at Bromley Squash Club; there was the usual buzz of anticipation and masses of friendly faces. Mike played the first round of the Over 45's in the morning and it was agony to watch. It looked like him on the court and yet it was not the real Mike. There was no sparkle, no bounce. The game was over very quickly and a very surprised opponent was through to the second round, the last thing he had expected. Mike went off to have a shower and I stayed on the balcony all alone. It was at that moment that I felt I knew what was wrong with Mike, and the horror of that realisation was too much to bear. A few people saw me crying and naturally jumped to the conclusion that it must be because Mike had lost, although knowing me, they were surprised. A very understanding player, whom I hardly knew at all, came over to me and asked if I would like a coffee. It was the last thing I wanted and yet it was good to have someone to talk to, except that I could not bring myself to voice my deepest fears. I blubbered about Mike not being well and awaiting some blood tests. The awful thing was that I knew that we had to go through the same thing again in the afternoon. I just wanted to take Mike away to spare him the embarrassment and his bewilderment. It was a repeat performance, only this time I vanished into the Ladies with my handkerchief.

A few very strange things happened over the next few days; Mike would be perfectly normal one minute and then he would look glazed and he would say something completely absurd and irrelevant. He came home from work one day with some Christmas cards that he had bought. He told me a really weird story about getting them free in some post office. I realised that he had actually no idea at all where he had got them from and was making up a story. I hoped that he had actually paid for them!

Our G.P. then rang to say that the blood tests were normal. He thought that he was giving me good news but all he got was sobs. I said that, in that case, there was something horribly wrong. I explained that earlier that morning I had debated taking Mike's car keys because I felt that he should not be on the road, but then he had seemed so normal at breakfast I had decided against it.

He listened to all this and said that if I could get Mike back straight away he would see him. I was able to contact Mike on his car phone and he agreed to come home and I said that I would meet him near the doctor's surgery. He took a very long time to arrive, by which time I was wondering what on earth to do, and our poor doctor was just waiting! Mike did not seem unduly concerned about being summoned back; he never really asked many questions about what was going on. Our doctor talked to him for a long time. I realised that Mike was often talking very convincing rubbish. I was seated behind Mike and would just nod or shake my head to give the doctor some idea of what was fact and what was fiction. He wanted Mike to have a scan to see if anything was going on inside his head, but as the waiting list to see a neurologist was ten weeks he decided that the best thing to do was for Mike to see a psychiatrist and he could then arrange the scan if he saw fit. We would only have to wait ten days for the appointment. Mike then latched on to the idea that he was to see a psychiatrist and wanted to know if that meant he was having a nervous breakdown. He was very cross about that!

Mike's friend, Pete Wiseman, had arranged to come and stay for the next weekend. He knew there were problems, but he was totally unprepared for what was to come. He was off on holiday to the Gambia the following weekend and wanted to see us before he went. He met us at the squash club. I was playing on court at the time so he chatted to Mike whilst they watched me. Mike asked what time the match at

Beckenham was the following Tuesday; Pete told him. Ten minutes later Mike asked him again and Pete told him again. This went on several more times and Pete became very puzzled and worried. Whilst I was showering and changing Pete and Mike went to the supermarket and bought some peanuts and crisps to eat before the meal. We arrived home and Mike sat down and ate the lot, leaving none for anyone else. This was totally out of character. His hunger was all consuming and nothing else mattered.

The meal was almost ready and Mike announced that he was going to have a bath! I gently pointed out that perhaps he could wait until after the meal, but no, off he went. Pete and I went into the kitchen and quietly talked together, both of us very worried about Mike's behaviour. I was just about to voice my deepest concerns when a sixth sense made me go out and check to see where he was. There he was, dripping wet, at the bottom of the stairs, with not a lot on, listening. In a moment of clarity he had wondered what was wrong with him and had decided to eavesdrop in the hope of hearing something. I never did tell Pete what I thought the problem was. We eventually sat down to eat and later moved into the living room for coffee. Mike promptly turned on the television, something he would never do if we had a visitor. I asked him why he had done it, he stared at me as if not seeing and said that one of our squash friends was about to appear on television. This, of course, was absolute rubbish and I am afraid I lost my presence of mind at that stage; I ran across the room, turned off the television and flung my arms around him and sobbed. Poor Pete, what a night out! We then went to bed, Mike slept like a baby, which is more that could be said for me.

Tuesday came and Mike still did not know what time the match was! Luckily, I did. He drove there, at one point misjudging a bend, and we narrowly missed an oncoming car. This was most unlike him and he apologised profusely. Mike went on court and lost very quickly to someone who would hardly expect to get a point off him. I was very nervous of being with people by this stage for fear of what Mike might say, so we left as soon as he had showered and I made sure that I was driving. On the way home, Mike looked across at me and asked if his father would be there when we got back. His father had been dead for ten years. He then seemed to realise what he had said and apologised for frightening me. Too right.

Mike drove to the office the next morning. I decided to follow in my car and after talking to his partner, persuaded Mike, with great difficulty, to leave his car behind and come home. He was very resistant at first but from that moment on he just accepted the fact that he was at home and not going to work. No questions asked.

We duly went to the psychiatrist who asked a lot of questions and prescribed some anti-depressants and said that he would arrange a brain scan at Midhurst in about two weeks time. The next fortnight was a nightmare. Mike was sleeping more and more and I was trying to carry on working myself in my treatment room downstairs. I felt that I had to make him get up late afternoon and have some exercise to keep him generally fit. He would wake up and tell me everything that he had done that day, all the calls he had made and the people he had seen. He seemed to have no idea that he had in fact been in bed asleep all the time. We would then go for a walk or into the town for a coffee and he would behave as if nothing were wrong. The strange conversations became more and more bizarre. I rang the psychiatrist and was just told to wait for the scan. It was very frightening, and I felt very alone.

It was at this stage that I started to find out what wonderful friends we had; Mike was such a popular person. I then felt less alone. We were asked out to dinner by some friends who knew that Mike might do something strange but they felt, rightly, that the outing would do us both good.

Mike's daughter, Karen, took a day off from work to come over and see him. She found it very hard to understand what was wrong, not surprising really. I found it impossible to explain. When she arrived everything seemed totally normal. They went for a walk together after lunch. On the way, Mike commented out of the blue on her love of football. She has always hated football! It was the first moment that she realised something was wrong, but it was so inexplicable.

The day arrived for the scan. Why it had to be at Midhurst, which is a very long way away, I do not know. The journey was horrific, every time we went through a town or village Mike would remember a customer, usually from the distant past, and say that we had to deliver something there. I would persuade him that this was not the case and after a short argument he would forget all about it until the next town and then the same thing would happen again. We stopped at a cafe for a coffee and I waited for him outside the gents because I knew that he had no idea where he was and might wander off. He was a model patient during the scan and behaved perfectly normally. I expect they very soon saw what was wrong, but no-one said anything. He has always been claustrophobic and I thought that he might find it terrifying, so I held his foot and talked to him all the time.

The journey back was not so bad; he just slept. I think he had forgotten all about the scan and thought we were just on our way back from somewhere.

The next day was a Friday. I was working as usual downstairs and Mike got up after lunch. The telephone rang and he answered it; he called through to me and I went and sat down next to him to take the call, having no idea who it was. It was the psychiatrist to tell me that he had the report on the MRI scan and that Mike had a brain tumour. He went on to say that it was cystic in appearance and they had arranged for him to be admitted to a neurosurgical ward the following morning. It was what I had suspected, deep down, all along, but what a way to be told. Mike was sitting beside me with no idea of what was happening, I had a patient in the next room and I had just found out that the most precious and loved man in my life was to have brain surgery for a tumour. I did think that, as a psychiatrist, he could have done better!

I politely thanked him, told Mike that it was his doctor on the telephone and went back to my patient. Poor lady, she had only been to me once before and knew nothing of what was going on in my life. Suddenly her physiotherapist dissolved into a useless heap. She was wonderful, she got dressed, took all the names and telephone numbers of the rest of my patients for that day and telephoned them herself to explain and cancel their appointments.

I collected myself and went back to Mike. I explained what had happened although he hardly seemed to understand. I then rang our G.P. who had no idea that I had been told; he sounded almost as upset as I did. I then found out that the hospital would need the scans and they had been posted in error to the psychiatrist. This would mean a long round trip in the morning to collect them before even starting to journey to London.

The telephoning and arranging that had to be done in order to tell friends and relations where we were, sort out my job and try to pack everything that Mike would need luckily took up most of the rest of that day, which was better than just sitting thinking about the horrors to come. I rang a friend whom I remembered lived near where the scans were going to arrive the following morning and she agreed to be there to collect them and bring them over to us before we left. That was a big logistical problem solved. That night seemed too short. I just wanted to hold Mike for as long as possible and not let him go; I had no idea if or when I would do it again. He started hiccuping a lot; I had noticed the odd one or two before but now it was almost constant. It was later explained to me that persistent hiccups in this situation usually indicate irritation within the brain.

Our friend, Gloria, arrived on schedule clutching the scans. She offered to drive us to London but I decided that it would be better to go alone so that I had my car with me and could stay if I wanted to. I had no idea where I would stay but I had packed a bag just in case. Getting a confused Mike up and dressed in time took some doing and the very worst moment was walking down the garden path and wondering whether he would ever walk up it again.

We found the hospital easily enough. It was one of the huge old Victorian workhouse variety with long concrete corridors and wards coming off it in two storey spurs. As we walked into the ward we had been told to go to I felt a sense of relief. For all those weeks I had known there was something very wrong but had to cope on my own, now Mike was "safe". I'd got him to the right place and now, hopefully, they would care for him and treat him. Mike was admitted by a young lady doctor, a very efficient and caring lady in whom I had every confidence. She asked me if I would like to look at the scans, something I had been too scared to do earlier. She put them up on the lit screen in her office and there it was, the huge offending item, slap bang in the middle of Mike's brain and about the size of a squash ball. I was absolutely horrified at the size. To think that it had been there growing without us knowing anything about it until recently.

Mike was totally submissive and co-operative and we were asked masses of questions. They have set questions for memory and it soon became apparent that Mike had lost his short term memory completely. It was explained to us, only Mike was oblivious, that the tiredness, the increased appetite and the memory loss were all exactly as they would expect, bearing in mind the site and size of the tumour. I was asked if he had vomited at all; the answer was no, but then, as if to prove me wrong, he did. This was an indication of the swelling in his head and it had just reached a critical point. Thank heavens we were at the hospital.

The last visit of the day was from the surgeon. He painted a very gloomy picture and explained that the tumour was far too large to be totally removed safely, so what he planned to do was to take away as much as was safe and then treat the rest with radiotherapy, having had a sample of it examined by the pathologist to see exactly what type it was. He planned to operate in about ten days time, in the meantime he would reduce the swelling immediately with steroids and arrange for masses of tests to be done to give as complete a picture as possible. He made no promises and after he had left I felt very empty and frightened for Mike. I knew he was in no state to make any decisions for himself, therefore it was up to me to give consent for everything to be done. An awesome responsibility.

I looked around the ward. It was called a high dependency unit so there were lots of nurses compared with the number of patients. The patients who were recovering from surgery, as Mike would be doing shortly, were attached to very high tech equipment and the standard of care seemed to be excellent. I knew we had no choice.

The surgeon actually gave me the choice of taking Mike back home with me that night as it was a Saturday and no more could be done until the Monday. It was explained to me that the steroids would take effect immediately and he would start to improve. Much as I loved him and much as I wanted him home, I had been so scared that day, realising how very ill he was that I wanted him in a safe environment. He was still so confused that I could see he would not be bothered either way, he was also very tired, so I decided to give him a shower and settle him for the night and then head for home. He was fast asleep before I left the ward so I felt sure I had made the right decision.

Then came the next problem; I had absolutely no idea how to get home and no map. Mike, despite everything, had managed to direct me to the hospital, but now I had to get back. It was almost Bonfire night so there were fireworks going off all around which did nothing for my nerves. I headed off in what I thought was approximately the right direction, unfortunately it wasn't. I came across areas of London I had never heard of. I just kept on driving. At one stage a car full of young men hooted and gesticulated at me for pausing to decide which way to turn. The next junction had bollards to 'calm' traffic and I managed to smile through the tears when they went at it so fast they had to stop and reverse before going through. As I was watching them make fools of themselves I saw a signpost to Dover and Folkestone which enabled me to find the right road. Perhaps they did me a favour after all.

The rest of the journey is a blur. I arrived home feeling completely hollow and numb. I had left the man I loved in hospital with a brain tumour, I had a lot of business and domestic sorting out to do, and I had no idea where to start.

I decided to start by ringing a colleague who had locumed for me before to see if she could take over my business. She had no idea of Mike's illness and although she was unable to help on the business side she said she was not going to let me be alone that night and would get straight in her car and come over.

The next problem was how to tell Karen, Mike's daughter. I decided that it would be too cruel to ring her at home so I rang a mutual friend who is a qualified nurse and works in the same company. She could tell her and be a shoulder to cry on at the same time. She also offered to stay the night!

The door bell rang about half an hour after I returned home. I could see through the glass that it was someone very tall with dark hair, to my surprise it was a squash friend of ours, Chris. He had heard via the grapevine about everything and had a get-well card for Mike. He and his fiancee lived in London and he was on his way back there but when he heard of my awful journey home he said that he would come back down the following morning, pick me up and show me the best route to take, and then bring me back the next evening. This seemed an awful lot of driving for him, but he wouldn't take no for an answer. He also insisted on staying until my friend, Pam, arrived for the night. The dreadful worry about Mike was still there, but the feeling of coping on my own had gone.

I was able to tell Pam the whole story and off-load, which helped. Then I went to bed and slept amazingly well. Breakfast turned into a very sociable feast as we were joined by Judy, the nurse who was going to tell Karen. Chris turned up, true to his word, and drove me to the hospital. Mike and I had not spent a night apart before and I was wondering how he would have taken it. I need not have worried. He had slept since I had left him and had not even noticed my absence. Chris came in and explained that he had brought me up. Looking faintly puzzled, Mike said not to worry about the return journey as he would take me home. I knew that this was impossible and assumed that Chris realised too; unfortunately he had not.

I spent the day caring for Mike and starting to adjust to the hospital routine. I had no idea how long this was to go on for, or that I would be with him for most of the time. The amazing thing was that I did not get bored at all, I just became bound up in the way of life. The nursing staff were fantastic, they made it clear that they would be there whenever required but if I wanted to do all the nursing of Mike they were perfectly happy for me to do so. I remembered the premonition I had had all those years before.

I helped Mike with his meals; eating was not a problem as his appetite was still voracious. I recall the soup which turned up for every meal - same flavour, sometimes a slightly different colour, but always with a different name! It was very difficult for me to eat as I never wanted to leave Mike's side. I would wait until he nodded off and then dash to the cafeteria for a sandwich. There was a 'quiet time' after lunch when the patients would have a sleep and no visitors were allowed. I would sit silently by the bed and was never asked to leave. I suppose as I was not disturbing anyone, Mike was one patient less to have to watch over.

The day passed remarkably quickly and I gave Mike a shower, settled him for the night and waited for Chris to come and collect me. No Chris! The awful truth dawned on me - he had believed Mike when earlier in the day he had said he would take me home. Poor chap, he had not known quite what to do so was waiting at his home just in case. He duly came for me and his fiancee had a meal ready for me at their flat before he took me home. The two of them had already taken on their roles during our problems. Chris became the "driver"; he was to chauffeur many people without cars to see Mike over the next few months and drive Mike and I when required. I am not at all sure what I would have done without his help. His fiancee would always come with him, but stay in the background because the number of visitors was limited. At the end of visiting she was there to comfort me. Chris also had the task of telling Mike's friend Pete when he came back from his holiday. He rang and arranged to meet him for a drink the following lunch time.

I drove back to the hospital on my own the next morning, thankfully with no geographical hitches. I went onto the ward only to find Mike's bed empty. The staff explained that the steroids were starting to work and he was much better so they thought it would be beneficial for him to be on a more ordinary ward until his operation. This was on the floor above. I ran up the stairs and found his new bed, but still no Mike; only this time no-one knew where he was. I panicked. A few minutes later he re-appeared; he had been looking for me and it sounded horribly as if he had been right out onto the main road in his dressing gown. The amazing thing was that he had found his way back - the drugs must have been doing something, there was no way he would have done that two days before.

It was to be a week of tests and I realised that I would have to find things for Mike to do to keep his mind occupied as he was so much more alert. I took in a board game and a pack of cards and we also did a simple crossword every day. I wanted to capitalise on this new found brain activity. There was at least one major test every day: a C.T. scan, an electro-encephalograph, a lot of visual tests, a neuro-psychological test and many blood tests. Visitors also started to appear as word got around. The days were becoming quite full and in between visitors and medical tests we would stroll around the hospital and often have a coffee in a canteen. This could have felt like quite a normal activity except for the fact that, on the nurses' request, Mike was wearing a track suit. He has always hated track suits and refused to wear them. We therefore had a cupboard full of the ones he had been given during his sporting career. The most comfortable one had 'England' on the back and dated from one of the times he captained the England side. I was a bit reluctant to use that one! We discovered a few quieter little nooks and crannies where we could have some privacy so we would often go there. It was a very strange week and it became harder to cope with, from my point of view, as the week progressed and the steroids took more effect. Mike became much more aware of what was going on and why he was there. Understandably, he was terrified.

Whilst we were at the hospital our friends were setting up three communication networks. Chris, after breaking the news to Pete, set about telling all Mike's friends in the squash world in and around London, and they knew they could ring him for news. The same thing started to happen in Brighton with a chap called Tony from the squash club there; he made sure he was up to date and then people could ring him. Similarly, in our hometown, a mutual friend, Mary, took on the communication role. This took a lot of the pressure off me. Even so I would often return home to an answering machine loaded with a dozen concerned messages. It was lovely to know that so many people cared and wanted to help but quite impossible to find the time, in the only hour that I had at home every day, to ring everyone back. I only hope that people understood.

One of the tests Mike had to undergo was a series of eye tests. These were to be done at a different hospital about five miles away. The normal procedure would have been for Mike to have gone in an ambulance with several other patients and then, when they had all finished, they would have come back together. I offered to drive him there myself and the staff were agreeable. It was a gruelling day for Mike. They did so many tests that required all his concentration. I was so glad when they had finished that I could just drive him back rather than wait around for the other patients to finish. The consultant ophthalmologist did a very efficient job but hardly communicated with us at all. He reminded me, visually, of 'Chalky' in the Giles cartoons.

My son, Nick, came down for one of the days during that week. He was doing a post-graduate course at Cambridge. The staff at his college were fantastically understanding and he became a tower of strength for me. Not only was I worrying and caring for Mike, but my younger son, Chris, was also ill and in need of my maternal care which I could not give him, being unable to cut myself in two! Nick came and helped me and then went over to his brother. Over the next couple of months Nick became the one person who seemed totally able to cope with Mike, however ill he was, and he never panicked or 'talked down' to him, he would just chatter away quite normally and do what needed to be done.

The doctors had completed all of Mike's investigations by the end of the week and had a fairly comprehensive picture of what was going on inside his head. They suggested that we go home for a long weekend before the operation which was scheduled for the following week.

One of the things Mike likes most of all is eating out in a nice restaurant, so I decided that we would do that every day and try to actually enjoy the weekend. His perception of what was about to happen to him was strange - he seemed to partially understand and be very frightened about it for short periods of time, and then he would forget and enjoy what we were doing at the time. It was so wonderful to have him home again, but so terrifying to think of what was to come.

The nurses had spoken to me about the best way for me to cope. The general consensus was that relatives managed better if they carried on working. That might be right for ninety per cent of the people that they encounter, but I knew that it would not be right for me. If I did carry on working, my mind would hardly be on my job and therefore it would not be right for my patients. Also, I knew that I wanted to be completely free to be with Mike and able to care for him without any other responsibilities. I therefore handed over to a locum and arranged for him to come into our house and treat my patients. It suited him as he was just starting up in private practice and it certainly suited me.

Chapter 3

EARLY NOVEMBER

Driving Mike up to the hospital for his operation was infinitely worse than the previous week. I felt as if I was taking a lamb to the slaughter. I had persuaded him to have the operation although he really had no idea of what he was consenting to. What if it all went horribly wrong? Would that be my fault? On the journey we talked very positively about what we would do for his convalescence. We decided to go to a really smart hotel in Bath. I thought that if everything went really well we might even be there in three weeks time. That thought helped us both. It was a very good job that we did not know what the situation would really be in three weeks time. That day seemed unnecessarily long because one of the doctors always insisted on his blood tests being done at nine in the morning. We had therefore to get up at the crack of dawn, do battle with the rush hour traffic and then face a long day doing nothing just to satisfy his request.

I arranged for Mike to have a portable television for that day and night to help to pass the time and, if possible, take his mind off what was happening. I was told that there was a room available for relatives of critically ill patients in what was called 'The Flat'. This was rationed to only three nights, so I decided that I would make that the three nights after the operation.

We were sitting together, just talking about everything except what was about to happen, when we saw a lady come into the ward. She was wearing a dog-collar and clutching a clip board. We deduced that she must be the chaplain. We are both Church of England but somehow did not feel like talking to her at that moment. We pretended not to see her. Undeterred she headed straight for us. The moment she arrived she dropped the clip board and papers went everywhere, she uttered an epithet that I did not expect to hear from a chaplain and funnily enough this made me realise that she was very human and I did want to talk to her. She stayed and talked for ages, about everything except religion, and this was how it was to be for the whole of our stay at the hospital. She was always there when we needed her, but she never pushed religion. She also told me that the little Chapel which was next to the ward could always be used by relatives as a quiet refuge. I certainly took up that offer over the next few weeks.

The next person to come and see Mike was the surgeon, plus entourage. I got the impression that he is a man who finds unpleasant things difficult to say, so rather than say them kindly with perhaps a little glimmer of hope to cling to, he gives you the very worst scenario, undiluted, full in the face, for you to absorb and cope with in front of his team of doctors and nurses. He told us that Mike might not survive and if he did he could well be brain damaged. He explained that the tumour was in the worst possible place - "right on the clockwork" as he put it. I suppose that he had to do it his way; we had to be warned but it was not easy to let Mike sign the consent form that was put in front of him. The entourage moved off leaving two desperately unhappy people in its wake. Mike was well enough by this time to have understood what he had just been told. He begged me not to go home that night but to stay in the hospital.

I waited until the ward was quiet again and I went to talk to the ward sister. She had heard it all and was wonderfully understanding. She promised to make some telephone calls and see if a room could be arranged. We did not want to go back into the ward so we went into the ward kitchen where the tea lady was preparing the tea trolley. She said things like "where there's life there's hope" and fed us someone else's pink birthday cake. I know that she said it to help, but it somehow sounded pessimistic to me. There was Mike looking very well and he might be dead by that time tomorrow. I never want to eat pink birthday cake ever again.

Another weird thought had just entered my mind - Mike and I had often joked about how often we looked at our digital clocks and they said eleven eleven. We had even asked ourselves if this meant anything. Mike was to have his operation on the eleventh of November. I decided against pointing this out to him.

My room in the 'flat' was duly organised and I went there with Mike. There was a front door which opened onto a small corridor with a bathroom leading off. There were about three doors with their own locks. My room was small but very adequate; a bed, chair, basin and, most important of all, a telephone which would give me a direct line to his ward. This little room was to serve it's purpose admirably. I had somewhere to sleep that was only five minutes walk down the corridor to Mike's ward and I felt in contact at all times. There must have been other people staying there because I heard comings and goings, but I never saw anyone else. It became my home and sanctuary for the next six nights, the hospital agreeing to extend my stay beyond the normal three day ration. It also gave Mike and I some much appreciated privacy on that dreadful day; we just lay down on the bed and cuddled, and I savoured every moment of it. All too soon we realised that Mike should be back on the ward to see the anaesthetist, so reluctantly we went back.

There was a visitor waiting by the bed. The ward sister had appreciated our need for time on our own and had pretended not to know where we were. This visitor had just spoken to the chaplain, who had told him the story, so he was struggling to look cheerful when we walked in. He did very well. He is a likeable cockney and he was soon chattering on about everything and nothing and taking our minds off the impending situation.

What a ghastly evening. I knew that it was in nobody's best interests for me to stay in the ward with Mike, especially as they had gone to the trouble to arrange my room, but I did not want to go. I eventually tore myself away and left him with his television turned on. As I walked out of the ward I did not dare look back. It seemed a very long and lonely walk up the cold concrete corridor and across the car park to my room. All night I wanted to go back and be with Mike, but if he had actually managed to sleep that would be a very unhelpful thing to do. I gave up on the idea of sleeping at about six in the morning and went back to the ward. A friend of mine, Stella, had arranged to come up from Brighton to be with me during the operation. That must be the definition of true friendship!

Poor Mike was wide awake and very frightened when I arrived. It was explained to me that they are unable to give any kind of pre-med to relax a patient before brain surgery as they need to be able to rouse them and assess their mental state as soon as possible. This made it a very long morning indeed. I gave Mike a long luxurious shower and washed his hair. I knew that it was to be shaven off in the theatre, but

I still wanted it to be clean. There was nothing else to do then except try to keep talking and wait for the dreaded sight of two porters and a trolley. Mike said that he wanted me to be with him for as long as possible and to go as far as the theatre with him. I agreed, but knew that this was going to test my self control to the limits. He then said that he wanted to wake up after the operation and see my smiling face - I'd do my best.

The lady Chaplain must have realised our needs and appeared just at exactly the right moment, and talked about everything from the ordination of women to her family. I really heard very little but was very grateful for her presence.

Then the sight that we had been dreading appeared: two very jolly porters and a trolley. They pushed Mike while I walked beside them holding his hand. We went up a steep, bleak corridor and through the swing doors into the theatres. This was as far as I was allowed to go. I had to kiss Mike good-bye and try a cheery "see you later" before I walked out. There was a little alcove halfway down the corridor and there I stayed until I had regained a measure of composure. Mike had also asked me to promise not to leave the hospital whilst he was having his operation, not that I would have wanted to anyway. I went back to my little room to wait for my friend Stella to arrive.

They telephoned me from the ward to tell me that Stella had arrived, at exactly the time I was expecting her, and I went down to meet her. She was fantastic, and being a doctor she could help by saying that the risky part could be inducing the anaesthesia and as we had heard nothing after the first hour, that was obviously good news. She had hoped that we could go for a walk - it was a lovely autumn day - or go to a pub for lunch. Both of these were impossible because of my promises to Mike, so it was the hospital canteen. I really do not know how we passed the day, but we did. It would have been quite unbearable without anyone to talk to.

We started to telephone the ward at mid-day - no news, two o'clock - no news, four o'clock - nothing. No-one could tell us anything. I think I must have been becoming quite impossible by then. We rang again at five and still there was no news. I decided to have a bath; it might relax me, and Stella could sit by the phone. I should think she was glad to have a few minutes break from my pacing up and down. At six thirty we decided to go to the ward rather than keep ringing. Mike had just been brought back.

He was in a cot-style bed by the door with a monitor screen beside him displaying his oxygen level, pulse and blood pressure. His head was in what looked like a huge white turban. Stella studied the monitor and said that it all looked good - it looked horrendous to me. He appeared to be semi-conscious and doing as requested. I realised immediately that although he could move his left side, it was weak. Not surprising, I told myself, as they had gone in through the right side of his brain and there would obviously be some swelling. I just wanted to sit quietly with him so that he would know I was there if he opened his eyes. Stella waited outside and I realised that the Chaplain had come along and she was talking to her. She must have stayed on at the hospital in case we had needed her - what a lady!

I felt that I could now cope on my own and I wanted Stella to get back to Brighton before too late. She was going via my son Chris to see how he was and tell him the news.

It was not long after she left that Mike seemed to turn to look at me, then his eyes rolled and he had a fit. I shouted and the nurses were there immediately and I was gently guided into the nurses office and a cup of tea put into my hands. I could hear a lot of commotion outside and I asked a young nurse if he was still alive; she replied "at the moment". Things quietened down and I was allowed back in, but in no time at all it happened again. This really terrified me; back into the nurse's office again. The night staff had come on duty by this time and they were fantastic. The sister came and sat down with me and explained that this often happened after brain surgery and the best thing that I could do was to go to my room and try to get some sleep. They said that I could come back at any time through the night if I wanted to, or ring the ward. They promised to ring me if anything happened. I knew this was the right thing to do, so, obediently, I went. I slept until five thirty and I rang the ward straight away, hoping that the absence of a telephone call from them was good news. The ward sister told me that he was much brighter and had just said "where's Brenda". I could not get dressed quickly enough and I ran down the deserted and still dark corridors. In the ward the lighting was very subdued but I was aware of activity around Mike's bed. I think that he had had non-stop attention throughout the night. I was allowed in - they never made me feel as though I was in the way. I asked if I could give Mike his morning wash and they agreed. There were a lot of tubes and leads in the way, but I managed. One of the connections was to Mike's thumb and this measured his blood oxygen level and pulse. He kept taking it off and this would sound an alarm in the nurse's office. He never gave them any chance to forget him! They would come and do various observations at very regular intervals to monitor his level of consciousness.

I knew that we would be the first port of call for the ward round so I waited eagerly for the sight of the surgeon. I wanted to hear exactly what they had done and how successful it had been. When he did appear he looked absolutely dreadful - very tired and not at all happy. He came straight in and told me the bad news. He had tried and tried to get to the tumour, but had failed completely. He thought he might have just touched something hard and had tried to get a nibble at it to send to the pathologist, but in all honesty he felt that all he had got was some brain tissue. Mike's precious brain tissue, I thought; perfectly good brain cells had been sucked up and put in a bottle. I was horrified. I wondered what function they had performed and if he would miss them. The surgeon explained that access to the tumour site was very restricted and any deviation either way could have been fatal. He had taken away a plate of bone on the right side of Mike's head and gone in that way. He said that when he realised that he was not going to succeed he had made the decision to stop rather than be too cavalier and possibly do Mike irreparable harm. He explained that he had inserted a 'shunt' which was two thin pipes into the fluid filled cavities of the brain with a plastic reservoir under the skin on the top of his head. It was explained that this was not actually doing anything but if, at a later date, it needed to be connected up to a vein in the neck to drain fluid off the brain, at least the 'donkey work' had been done. He said that it was "most unfortunate" that Mike had had the fits as this would make the brain swell even more and impede his recovery. He predicted a "stormy period" ahead.

Because he had been unable to reach the tumour they still did not know what sort it was and so they were actually no wiser than they had been the previous day. He said that there were probably three options. One was that it was very benign and therefore completely insensitive to radiotherapy. He favoured this diagnosis because it had felt so hard. Where did that leave Mike, I wondered? Another option was a nasty vicious thing that would respond quickly to radiotherapy but would need drugs as well and would probably quickly recur - thanks! And the third option was something called a cranio-pharyngioma which is what the radiologist who had first seen the scan had thought. This was far and away the best option, being very slow growing and possibly radio-sensitive. The trouble was that no radiotherapist would want to do the radiotherapy without a definitive diagnosis. He therefore talked of another operation when Mike was well enough; a stereotactic biopsy, whatever that was. Then he walked away. I had to feel sorry for him - he had done his best but had achieved nothing. I desperately wanted him to give me a small shred of good news or some tiny fragment of hope on which to cling. But no, nothing, just nothing.

It was the same situation as two days previously, only at least this time Mike was unaware of what had been said and it's implications. The nurse pulled the curtain around Mike's bed and left us in peace. I clung to his hand in silence. I could hear the ward round as it continued to go from bed to bed. Eventually all was quiet. I looked out and the only person in the nurses office was the young lady doctor, the one who had admitted Mike in the first place. I went in to her. She was obviously upset as well. I said that I wanted some good news, it did not have to be a lot (I knew that would be asking too much). I said that I just had to have something that I could hope for. She said that all she could say was that the surgeon had done no harm, he had stopped in time. I went back to the bed and told myself that this at least should mean that when the effects of the operation wore off we should at least only be back to square one. Looking at Mike, this was very hard to believe. I studied him closely. I was not at all sure of how much sight he had. When he looked at me he turned his head most oddly, his right eye was so swollen it looked as if he had just lost a boxing match, and the left one did not appear to be functioning very well. I tested his left side for movement, he was responding to my commands as best he could, but the muscles seemed to be very weak indeed. The good news was that he definitely knew who I was and told me how much he loved me. He never asked what had happened to him.

Chapter 4

THE STORMY PERIOD

I was very pleased that our friend Jill was coming up to see us that day as I desperately needed someone to talk to, and someone with more medical knowledge than myself to translate some of what I had been told. When she arrived she had brought a large bag of grapes because she knew that Mike would need plenty of fluids, and this was a nice tasty way to get them. We sat beside him and carefully peeled, cut in half and de-pipped every one. Mike appeared to thoroughly enjoy them and then when we looked at his face he looked as though he had mumps, then we realised that he had not swallowed them - he was like a hamster, with the grapes stored in his cheeks. It dawned on us that although able to swallow, he had to be told to do so, it did not come automatically. This situation remained for several days; I would give him food, let him chew it and then say "swallow". The nurses had given me some little sticks with lemon flavoured wet tips for cleaning out his mouth; he would take them from me and suck them like lollipops. The one bit of good news was that he did not seem to have any perception of pain at all and seemed quite content with his lot. If he had been in distress, it would have been too awful.

The various tubes and wires were gradually disconnected over the next two days. The first thing to go was the oxygen mask, this had been so regularly removed by Mike anyway, but at least it was thought to be no longer necessary. The monitor on his thumb, which had also spent more time off than on, was also removed. The remaining problem was the bandage on his head and a drain into one of the wounds, all of which was in jeopardy if you took your eyes off him for a moment. In fact, he did eventually take the whole lot off and remove the odd stitch without apparently feeling any pain. I had been warned that brain tumours and any kind of brain trauma such as surgery could produce a personality change with possible aggression and I was not to be upset if this happened. It never did. Underneath all the bandages and bruising, it was still my Mike, as loving as ever.

Jill stayed all of that day, she sat with Mike whilst I went to get myself something to eat. Eventually, she had to go in the early evening and I wondered if we would have any more visitors. Apparently, Chris had arranged to bring Pete over. Poor Pete, he could hardly bear to come into the ward. The last time he had seen Mike was on the eventful weekend at our house. Mike opened the one available eye and said "it's young Wiseman" and went to sleep again. They didn't stay long, but it was wonderful to feel their support and friendship. Heather was waiting outside for them and gave me a long, very much appreciated cuddle when they left.

I did feel very alone after they had gone so I gave Mike a good wash before they put the lights down for the night. One of the nurses commented later that he was always the cleanest patient on the ward! I liked doing it, it was an act of love. Also, in my many years of working on hospital wards I had learnt to accept a certain smell and things like filthy finger nails. I vowed that Mike would always look and smell clean. He was probably actually a lot cleaner than I was as I had not expected to stay when I did and I was existing in one outfit of clothes and the contents of the overnight bag I had put in the boot of the car on our first trip up to the hospital. I desperately needed to get hold of a change of clothes and also some money. The hospital agreed to extend my stay in the flat to six nights, but what to do for clothes and funds?

I went back to my little room and decided to wash all my clothes in shampoo and dry them on the radiator. I had a very nice grey woollen jumper, size fourteen. By morning I had a sweet smelling, matted, size ten skinnyrib! It was a good job that I was losing weight! I was getting used to the ward routine fast. I would be on the ward before the night staff had gone off duty and would give Mike his morning drink. I had been told that he would have to take in two litres of fluid a day, and all of this had to be recorded and matched against output, balancing the books as Nick put it. This was a simple job to do and one less for the nurses. They would come round very regularly and do the neurological observations, the usual temperature, pulse, respiration and checking limbs for movement (which remained very weak on the left side) plus a battery of questions. First they would ask Mike where he was - no chance, when his birthday was - he usually got that right, then what day of the week it was. I never knew myself so I was hardly surprised when he didn't. He had a one in seven chance of getting it right! Then they would ask who I was, this always amazed him. He always got that one right, to my enormous relief. The last question was very interesting, with the benefit of hindsight. It was "who is the Prime Minister". I now realise that when Mike was at his worst and his brain was very swollen he would say "Harold Macmillan", and as he got better he worked his way up to the present day and "John Major". His short term memory was non-existent but he remained totally accurate with his memories of the past. We would still do the quick crossword every day and he was as good as ever. I realise now that he did not truly know who

I was, or how I had come into his life, he just knew my name was Brenda and that he loved me.

Our daytime visitor the next day was a friend of mine with whom I had trained many years before. She had made a long and difficult journey by train from Southampton. She is the sort of friend I see very rarely, but if I am ever in trouble she will just down-tools and come to my rescue. She, like most people, thought that I should get out and have a break, but I just didn't want to. I compromised and left Mike for the time it took us to have lunch in the hospital canteen - not exactly what she had in mind, but it was as far away from Mike as I was prepared to go. I also walked as far as the main gate of the hospital to say goodbye to her, then rushed back to Mike. In the evening Mary and her husband, Alan, came up from Tunbridge Wells. They had decided not to come in to see Mike but to see me and do whatever they could to support us. They figured that, in the long run, the most helpful thing for Mike was to keep me propped up and functioning. They were armed with a huge box of chocolates for me which Nick and I demolished the following day. I wanted them to see Mike, so reluctantly they went onto the ward. Mary was amazed, there was Mike, obviously very sick and bandaged, he opened his eyes and said "hello Mary, hello Alan, how's Nick"? Nick is their son and an old squash friend of Mike's until he developed anorexia nervosa. Mary was overcome. Here was Mike, so desperately ill, asking after Nick. At this point Mike was sick and there was a lot of blood. Poor Mary and Alan! The nurse came and Mike apologised profusely to everyone for causing embarrassment. I thought this was a very worrying event, but the medical staff came up with some plausible explanations which I chose to believe. Mike's bed was one up the ward from the door at this stage and I knew that he would be moved up the ward with progress and nearer the door with any retrograde steps. They did not move his bed, so I decided that it really was nothing to worry about.

When I arrived the next morning Mike had been moved to the middle of the ward. This was real promotion in my eyes, so I was delighted. Nick arrived during the morning. He had not seen Mike since the operation but was perfectly able to cope with what he found. I left him to give Mike his lunch which gave me a chance to eat properly. I came back to hear Nick commenting that it was a good job there was no pattern on the hospital plates, otherwise he was sure that Mike would have scraped it off! He also checked Mike's fluid chart, chided him for not 'balancing the books' and gave him another drink. Mike had caused great amusement in my absence. There was a patient at the other end of the ward who was rather deaf. He was being asked the usual questions including "when is your birthday"; Mike heard this and answered "23rd November". The patient had not heard so was asked again, this time Mike looked a little surprised and answered rather louder. On the third time Mike shouted "didn't you hear me, 23rd November". This brought a little laughter into an otherwise sombre ward.

I was extremely glad to have Nick with me that day because I knew it was very likely that Karen would be coming to see her father. I hoped that she would not be alone. I was used to how Mike looked by this stage and Nick, probably with all his doctor friends and a physiotherapist for a mother, had not seemed too shocked, but Karen would never have seen anything like it before and it was her beloved father. We had tried to prepare her by saying that he might have two black eyes and a shaven head. In fact he had one black eye and the remains of a large bandage on his bald head, although he had made a good job of removing most of it himself already!

It was Nick who spotted her, she was standing alone at the end of the ward, absolutely rooted to the spot with tears running down her face. I rushed over to her and gave her a hug and tried to tell her all the good news I could think of. I guided her over to Mike - luckily he was awake and recognised her straight away, which must have helped. Sitting with him was more than she could cope with, so on the pretext of needing a drink she and Nick went off together and chatted about everything that Nick could think of until she felt ready to come back again.

After Karen had left, Nick and I talked about Mike's brother, David. I had kept him informed of events and expected him to visit, but he had not appeared, which puzzled me. Nick offered to ring him again and stress how ill Mike actually was. He then left to stay with his brother Chris and see how he was getting on after his illness.

I was left alone on the ward. The evenings on the ward were strangely active, yet peaceful. All the other visitors had gone by eight, but no-one ever asked me to go. I would just sit quietly beside Mike's bed and read the same paragraph of my book over and over again, do anything he needed and just watch the events in the ward. I felt almost invisible, like a fly on the wall. Eventually I went back to my room. I walked up the long corridor and past the porter's lodge. It was then about a hundred yards across the car park to the entrance of the 'flat'. It was in the car park that I became aware of being followed. I realised that if someone undesirable came into the flat with me nobody would have any way of knowing. I quickly got my key ready and, at the last minute, I ran as fast as I could, turned the lock, ran in and slammed the door behind me. I told myself that I was probably being stupid and imagining things. The next day I was told about a convict who had escaped from the guards on his ward the previous evening by climbing through a lavatory window. I went cold - what if he had forced his way in behind me?

The following morning, the curtains were drawn around Mike's bed when I arrived and a nurse's voice was saying "oh Mike, if you weren't so lovely I'd be cross with you". Apparently the cot sides of the bed were puzzling Mike; he had no idea what they were doing there and so if he wanted to get out of bed, having no concept of his inability to stand or walk, he would try to climb over them and get himself in an awful tangle. When he was told off he looked like a naughty schoolboy and said that he was terribly sorry. The trouble was that he then forgot all about it and in a matter of minutes would be doing the same thing again! It then dawned on me why the nurses were so glad to have me around, otherwise they needed eyes in the backs of their heads at all times.

The physiotherapists had been asked to see Mike. I was not at all sure about this. Being a physio myself I had been quietly doing what I thought appropriate. I had moved Mike's legs and encouraged him to exercise them himself regularly. I had made sure he did breathing exercises to keep his lungs clear. I knew that walking would be impossible because of the weakness on his left side so I had been sitting him on the side of the bed with his feet on the floor and tried to improve his balance. In order to stand we looked as though we were on the ballroom floor, but it was safe and helped him to take weight through his left side in a secure way.

They arrived and I just sat and watched. Maybe I am being hard on them, but I felt it achieved nothing to drag Mike across the ward by his armpits in an attempt to walk him, whilst gravity did it's worst with his pyjama trousers. I rushed over, rescued Mike from the total indignity of losing his trousers and then I went into the nurses office because I could bear it no longer. I explained my point of view to the nurses and they agreed with me. Thereafter, every time the physios appeared, someone would make an excuse for why Mike was not available for treatment. They soon got the message. I feel very strongly that a patient's dignity should always be respected, and it wasn't. I also knew that we had plenty of strong, willing, squash playing visitors whom I could persuade to help me whilst I did the treatment myself.

I put that plan into operation the same afternoon. The first 'willing' visitor was Pete, the amiable cockney who had last seen Mike the night before the operation. I explained my plan to him, pulled the curtains around the bed and taught him how to support one side of Mike whilst he sat on the side of the bed and tried to learn how to balance. Poor Pete, he had never thought of himself as a physiotherapist helper, but he did very well. The nurses peeped around the curtain and were highly amused!

Mike was starting to hiccup a lot more; they were huge, noisy hiccups that could be heard from outside the ward in the corridor. They must have been most uncomfortable for Mike and very disruptive for the rest of the ward. He also slept a lot and when he was asleep there was no rousing him. Then, as if a switch had been flicked, he would wake up. Otherwise the only way to wake him was to put the smell of food under his nose, this always worked! He was asleep (and hiccuping) later on that afternoon and I was sitting beside the bed when

I saw a man at the end of the ward whom I did not recognise.
He started to walk towards us, looking very shaken. He
obviously knew Mike. Not knowing who he was I gently
walked to the end of the ward with him to explain the
situation. Poor chap, he was a very old farming friend of
Mike's who had been told that Mike had had an operation,
but he had not been forewarned of the severity. He then
plucked up courage to come back to the bedside, obligingly
Mike woke up at that moment and recognised him which
eased the situation considerably.

Chris and Pete Wiseman visited that evening and Mike slept
the whole time. Pete described him as being as bald as a
billiard ball, an apt description. Pete had brought him a
present of a tie, it was a lovely tie - vivid green and purple
stripes, but looking at Mike lying there I could never imagine
him wearing a suit and tie again. I put it to the back of the
cupboard and tried to forget about it.

The next morning I arrived on the ward to find Mike already
washed and shaved. The nurses said they felt very guilty
about it, but Mike had specifically asked, so, quite rightly,
they had gone along with his request. I felt deprived, although
I knew that this was most unreasonable. They really were
very kind. One of the nurses used the word "sausage" as a
term of endearment for the patients. That day she came up
to Mike and said "come along sausage". A rather peeved
little voice said "I'm not a sausage"!

Mike did seem a lot brighter and his balance had improved
to the point where it was practical for him to walk to the
toilet with the ward sister and myself. He really was taking
proper steps; I was delighted. We had just arrived at our
destination when a nurse, looking rather amazed said that

there was a call for me in the office from Hong Kong. I just had to leave the sister and Mike and answer it. It was my friend, Sue. She had spent a week telephoning England and talking to everyone she could think of before she had managed to track us down. She is a very close friend and she had realised something was amiss when I sent her birthday card a month early! She had managed to piece together most of the information and realised how serious it all was, and she was ringing to ask if I would like her to fly home. What a wonderful offer. I declined but it left me with a nice warm feeling that she should even suggest it. I then remembered Mike and the sister. They were beginning to wonder when I would return, but were having a good chat!

Along with Mike's improvement with the walking came more ability to feed himself. There was always a salt and pepper pot on the tray. That day he took the salt and shook it frantically into the soup. In a way this was understandable, at least this would give it some kind of flavour, but it did seem rather excessive. Later in the day a doctor came round to say that the blood tests that morning had shown a very reduced sodium level. It was as if his body had tried to correct this deficit. Now we had to reduce his fluid intake rather than push in the two litres.

I was told that the stereotactic biopsy would probably be towards the end of the next week because Mike was progressing so well. I was glad that it was going to be done and yet dreaded Mike losing all the progress that he had made.
Nick arrived again that day. He was there when I needed him but in between, or if we had other visitors, he went back to my room to study or go into the visitors room to watch sport on the little black and white television there. This was

a horrid little room, very functional. There were a few chairs and some very old magazines, but I suppose that any relatives from that ward would not care what sort of reading matter was available as they would only be half reading it anyway. There was a kettle, some mugs and milk and the various people who used the room made sure that there was coffee. Some relatives slept in there and I realised how lucky I was to have had my room. Unfortunately, I had to vacate it that day so I was very pleased that I would have Nick to come home with me that night. Mike had a lot of visitors that day - he slept through the lot!

It seemed most strange to be leaving the hospital. I hated leaving Mike and yet I longed to see our little house, get some fresh clothes and sort out the post and answering machine. Nick suggested that we stop off for a meal. We did, but I felt really guilty, Mike so loved eating out and it was somewhere that he and I had often been to together. Poor Nick was deprived of a sweet, I just wanted to get away. I rang the ward as soon as we got home and then again first thing in the morning. Mike was alright. The pattern of life went back to leaving home after breakfast, driving up to the hospital and coming home again late in the evening with barely enough time to eat, sort out the post and do Mike's washing.

The weather was dreadful the next night. Not having listened to the radio, I had not heard the warnings against using the motorway. It was raining so hard that visibility was appalling and stopping would have been almost impossible. There seemed to be one motorcyclist and myself on the road and that was too many. I knew that I owed it to Mike not to have an accident, but it was jolly difficult.

The next day, totally unexpectedly, a young squash playing friend of Mike's from Brighton appeared on the ward. He is a very gentle, caring young man and as he left he leaned over and kissed Mike. He told me later that he never expected to see Mike again. Mike did seem to be deteriorating; his left side was slightly weaker and walking was once more impossible. He was sleeping a lot of the time, seemed more confused and was hiccuping again.

I was becoming more and more worried about the weakness in Mike's left side which seemed to be becoming worse by the hour. Jill arrived to visit during the late afternoon. We both checked him again and decided to alert the medical staff. They in turn called the surgeon and by the time he had arrived there was no movement at all on the left side and Mike's face had dropped on the one side again. The fear was that Mike was bleeding inside his brain and if that was the case he would have to be operated on straight away.

It was at this moment that Karen arrived. The poor girl looked as white as a sheet. They prepared Mike for a scan and the three of us, not knowing what to say to one another to cheer ourselves up, just sat in a very dejected line in the corridor. It all happened very quickly; the porters arrived and Mike was wheeled past, still in his own bed. He opened his eyes and waved cheerily at us with his right hand. We just had to sit and wait. Time was getting on, Karen had to catch a train back to her home, and I knew Mike would not want her on her own too late at night.

Jill had to drive back to Brighton and, unfortunately, had only just made it to the hospital with a very empty petrol tank. I had to drive home and none of us had eaten. Suddenly, the swing doors opened and Mike's bed reappeared with a fast asleep Mike in it. He was followed by a very relieved surgeon. Apparently the problem was swelling and not bleeding and so no operation was needed, just an increase in the steroids. He had also been able to admire his handiwork; the shunt was perfectly positioned! He started to explain everything to me but I knew that nothing was going in. I told him that Jill was a doctor and so if he explained it all to her in great detail, she could feed it back to Karen and myself in manageable portions. Jill went into the office and I could see them talking with the scans up on the screen. Jill came out, white and shaking. She blamed the heat but I was not convinced. The surgeon had said that Mike would never be the same again. He would, obviously, never play squash again as there was just too much damage to his brain.

We all stayed around for a few minutes, but as Mike was completely blotto we decided that the most sensible thing to do was to get us all home. Jill was very worried about me and wanted to get some food inside me before I drove home. I was worried about Karen and wanted to see her safely onto the train. We decided to drive her to the station and then come back to a restaurant near to my car and the hospital and have a very quick meal. This would have been quite a swift operation had Karen known the way; it was not her fault, the bus that she normally took was allowed to go where cars are not, and Jill's car was running on air. This all made for a lot of tension after all the strains of the evening. We drove round and round in circles with Jill's petrol gauge sitting firmly on empty. Eventually we found the station, Karen got out and cried all the way home and Jill and I went back to have a quick snack before setting off on our separate ways. The car did make it to a petrol station!

I rang the ward as soon as I woke the next morning to be told that Mike had improved slightly overnight. I then telephoned Karen. I felt that if there was already some recovery of movement on the left side, more would surely follow. The worrying part was finding Mike back in the bed nearest to the door - an indication of everyone else's concern. I had watched with such pleasure as he had progressed down the ward and here he was, back at first base again. I gently moved his left side and encouraged him to help me as much as he could. There was no movement in his hand but he was able to move the arm as a whole and there was a flicker of movement in his ankle. This was a vast improvement on the previous night. He was still very sleepy and hiccuping a lot. When asked who the Prime Minister was, he said "Harold Macmillan". Not a good sign.

They dimmed the lights on the ward as usual after lunch. I put one of Mike's spare pillows next to his head, sat down beside him and put my head on it and, lulled by the rhythmic hiccuping, we both slept for a couple of hours.

That evening Pete and Chris were the only visitors. Mike slept peacefully on and was unaware of anyone. I therefore decided to go home slightly early as it was a horrible rainy evening and I was feeling very tired. Pete and Chris said they would walk with me to my car as it was parked in a car park around the back of the hospital. They waited whilst I turned the engine on, then the wipers which emitted a dreadful grinding noise. I simply could not work out what was happening, then realised that I had no wiper blades, just the supporting rods that were rubbing on the windscreen. There was no way I could drive home like that, so I followed Chris's car with great difficulty to a garage. The three of us, all totally technically inept, attempted to fit the wiper blades.

It was actually very simple but we had all tried to make it complicated. At last I was able to drive home. So much for my early night! I wonder what sort of person goes around hospital car parks stealing windscreen wiper blades?

Sometimes, when I arrived home, I would find that my neighbour had left me a meal on the kitchen table. I really hoped that this would be the case, no such luck. I was reduced to a couple of stale rolls and some rather dried out cheese. Then the telephone rang, it was my neighbour to tell me that she had left me some food - pheasant casserole and spotted dick - a real feast. She had left it with a note saying "Brenda, thought you might like this, Ros!" My Locum's name was Brendan, you can guess the rest. Whatever made him think that my neighbour would leave him a meal?! He had returned the dishes and said that he hoped he would have room for the meal his wife would have waiting for him. Ros just took back the dishes, speechless. He was definitely not my favourite person at that moment.

I arrived at the hospital the next morning to find that Mike had been promoted and was now one bed up from the door. He was always so pleased to see me, but never really knew that I had been away. I gave him his morning wash and assessed the movement in his left side; it was definitely improving. There was even a flicker in the fingers. I decided that he was ready to start sitting on the side of the bed again to work on his balance and to take some weight through his left side. The nurses were great, they came and helped me. In response to their routine questions Mike said that Margaret Thatcher was the PM - this was better.

I drove home that night feeling much happier. Mike had stayed awake long enough for me to wash him and settle him for the night. It was still over a month until Christmas but near to our home they had put fairy lights in a large fir tree. Mike and I love Christmas and it brought it home to me that this was not going to be the same. I cried and cried. Thereafter I would take a different route in order not to see them.

The following morning I really thought that everything was against me - the washing machine flooded and fused all the lights. This was no big deal really, but on top of everything else it seemed like the last straw. Mike and I have a silly little ritual; if we see one magpie we say "Hello magpie" in order to avoid bad luck. Quite daft, but there you are! There were a lot of magpies around that year and I had been most remiss, I had not been through the ritual. There was often a single one in the same place and that morning I found it most therapeutic to call that solitary magpie every name under the sun and to blame it for all our misfortunes.

The goods news was that Mike had been moved even further down the ward, they must have been pleased with his progress. Then came the bad news, he was so much better and they needed his bed, so he was to be moved upstairs to the ward where he had been before. I was terrified for Mike. I knew that this was unreasonable because he had been there before and all the staff knew him, but there were fewer nurses to each patient and I wanted to feel that someone was watching him all the time. The nurse downstairs told me that strictly speaking he should have gone the previous day, it was only because they had become so fond of him that he had stayed. The one nurse who had been very responsible for Mike when he had been at his worst said that she would come upstairs to see him on his birthday which was in a few days time. I felt as though we were going a hundred miles away, not just upstairs. We hung on until a seriously ill patient needed the bed and then we had to go.

Everyone was aware of my anxiety and they suggested that Mike was put in the double side ward on his own. They were doing this to be kind but it actually made me even more worried because I felt that he would be seen less. The young lady doctor came around and I voiced my worries to her. She looked at the empty bed on the other side of the ward and went out of the room. A few moments later she came back in, grinning. She said that the ward sister had agreed to me sleeping in that bed for the night. This just seemed so wonderful, for the first time since his operation I was to be really close to Mike all night. I was thrilled.

When it actually came to it, it felt really weird. I was getting into bed in full view of the corridor in an NHS hospital, using the patients shower and toilet facilities, and yet I was not a patient. Apparently, when the night sister came round she was absolutely furious, but there was nothing that she could do, I was tucked up in bed and asleep. When I woke in the morning, I looked over to Mike, he smiled and waved at me as if it was the most normal thing in the world for us to be sharing a hospital ward.

Shortly after I had made the decision to stay the night at the hospital, I was called to the sister's office. Mike's brother was on his car 'phone; at last he was coming down to see Mike. He and his wife were in fact near our house but I had no intention of giving up my opportunity of staying with Mike. I told them who had a key and at least I could give them a list of things I wanted brought up.

I spent the next morning with a ball of string and sticky tape, hanging up all of Mike's 'get well' cards. He had masses and masses of them and by the time I had criss-crossed the room with string and hung the cards on them it looked positively festive. I then decided it was time to give Mike his physiotherapy. He was well enough to stand again in the 'ballroom dancing' position. This could be seen from the corridor and appeared to intrigue the other patients and their visitors.

The visitors poured in that afternoon, including Mike's brother and his wife. I then learnt the reason why they had not been before; another relative had been very ill. I was so involved in our little world that it had not occurred to me that other people have problems as well. They found seeing Mike very distressing; it was far, far worse than they were expecting. They stayed a short while and then left, very upset, to start their long journey back up North.

Another visitor that afternoon was Judy, a nurse. Whilst she was there Mike complained that his left calf hurt. We both looked at each other, the same thought in both our minds, was this a thrombosis? We examined his leg and sure enough it was swollen and tender at the back. This almost certainly did mean that he had a blood clot there, which is potentially life threatening because if a portion of the clot breaks off it could easily go to Mike's lungs. I immediately called the nurse and a doctor was summoned. He agreed that this was probably what it was, but it posed a medical dilemma. Ideally, Mike should be put on anti-coagulants to thin the blood, but this would not be a good idea so soon after brain surgery with the risk of bleeding into the brain. Catch 22. They decided to compromise and put him on a small dose and arranged a veno gram (to Xray the veins) the next day to confirm the diagnosis. I had to drive home that night not knowing if I would still have a Mike in the morning.

He did survive (if he were a cat, he must have been on about his fourth life). I went with him down to Xray. I held his hand as they injected a dye into a vein in his foot, this would then travel up his leg and give them a picture of the veins. I had to leave the room for my own safety whilst they actually did the Xrays. He was in a very coherent mood and asked the doctor what was wrong. It was explained to him, and a rather plaintive voice said "but I don't want to die". The radiologist put the venograms up on a screen and showed me. I did not like what I saw; there was no doubt at all about the diagnosis.

We went back to the ward and the awful implications of this new complication began to sink in. The most obvious was too dreadful to contemplate, so I mentally banned it from my thought process. The others were almost equally worrying. Mike's stereotactic biopsy was scheduled for the next week. He was now on anti-coagulants, albeit a low dose. There was no way they could do any further brain surgery now that the risks of bleeding were far too great. It would be too dangerous to take Mike off the drugs in order to have the operation, another Catch 22. The radiotherapist had said that he was not prepared to give Mike radiotherapy, which was the only hope of survival that Mike had left, without the definite diagnosis of what kind of tumour he was treating. I thought and thought about the problem and I could see no way over it except for a lot of persuasion of the consultant radiotherapist.

The way I saw it was that if the tumour was not radio-sensitive it would not respond, it would probably swell with the treatment which would make Mike worse and then it would just carry on growing, and that would be it - curtains. If it was the very virulent and nasty type, the radiotherapy would work quickly, they would spot this and be able to give Mike the chemotherapy as well. If it was the best option, the craniopharyngioma, it would slowly shrink after an initial swell. There was no decision to be made, I just had to persuade the doctors to 'go for it'.

Chapter 5

THE BIRTHDAY

The next day was Mike's 49th birthday. I had no idea what to get him so I had opted for a portable stereo which would mean that so long as someone else rigged it up, he could listen to his favourite music in bed. Karen had also wondered what to buy for him and I had suggested that she wait until Christmas when I hoped he would be better. She therefore arranged to have a wonderful, creamy sponge birthday cake made for him and had left it at the hospital. I also had a far inferior specimen made for him. So there was Mike, with his huge appetite and two enormous birthday cakes, absolute heaven! I did suggest that we cut the lesser one up and share it with the other patients and staff and Mike woefully watched as all his wonderful food left the room. It was difficult to ration his slices of Karen's cake. I'm quite sure that he would have happily devoured the lot in one sitting, given half a chance, which he wasn't! It was his birthday after all, so he did have a lot more than was probably good for him, but certainly not the entire cake. We opened his masses of birthday cards and strung them up as well as the 'get well' cards that were already there. Every day that passed reduced the risk of him having a fatal embolus from his deep vein thrombosis. I was beginning to believe that he was going to survive this latest threat.

The opportunity to speak to the doctors came the following day. I put my point of view to the surgeon who seemed very receptive and said that he would speak to the radiotherapist. To my enormous relief he agreed to do it. Suddenly it was 'all systems go'. There were a lot of discussions about which hospital Mike should be transferred to and we decided on one in Central London which had the most up to date equipment on site, so that all Mike would have to do each day would be to be wheeled downstairs. One option had been another hospital and an ambulance journey each day; I dismissed that. The bed was booked and an ambulance arranged for two days time. It was rather frightening. Again, I felt that I had made all these decisions on Mike's behalf, what was I letting him in for? We were to leave the hospital where he had been so well looked after for the last month and going off into the unknown.

The next day Mike seemed unwell again, this time he had a high temperature, so much so that they put a fan in his room. This really upset the rather miserable patient who was now occupying 'my' bed. He wanted the door and windows closed. If anyone dared to leave them open he moaned loudly. He seemed to be the sort of patient who complained about everything on point of principle. This was not the sort of person I wanted to share a room with my Mike, who was obviously not at all well. It was extremely difficult, after all the emotions of the previous few days, to keep my temper. Later on that day I heard him having a go at the doctors; at least it was not just us who incurred his anger. He then sat, wrapped in his dressing gown and blankets with his back to us, to make the point.

I think that everything just got to me that day, and when Mike had his afternoon nap the ward sister came in to find me sobbing. She invited me into the staff room and made me a cup of coffee. She then gave me one of the best bits of advice that I was to have. She told me off, kindly, for crying. She said that if Mike were aware of it he would feel the negative feelings and this would not help his recovery. On the other hand, if I could keep myself positive he would feel this and it would give him the strength to fight on. This made so much sense. I vowed to do my very best to think positive thoughts from that moment on; her words were etched on my mind. I went back into Mike, a much more optimistic person. I sat down beside him, put my head on his pillow and went fast asleep.

I awoke to see a familiar face looking at us through the glass partition. It was Bob, a very old friend of Mike's. He had driven up from Margate to see him, had found us both fast asleep and had just waited until we woke up. He was very upset when he saw Mike, my resolve not to cry vanished and we just hugged each other and sobbed in the corridor. We were helped, yet again, by the timely arrival of the chaplain. She said all the right things and we were all three talking cheerily beside Mike's bed when Karen arrived. Mike may have been very ill, but he still recognised everyone and thoroughly enjoyed their visits. It became apparent later in the day that the possible reason for Mike's temperature was a stomach upset. Nobody seemed unduly concerned, so I stopped worrying and just started thinking about our change of abode and how it was going to affect us. My poor mother, who was feeling very isolated and out of touch was due to come up with Jill the next day. I decided to postpone this, the journey to Central London would actually be a lot simpler for her.

The last day at that hospital was spent packing all of Mike's accumulated belongings ready for an early departure by ambulance the following morning. The light relief was at lunchtime when his visitor was the Chairman of Kent Squash. He fed Mike his lunch and commented that he had not expected to spoon feed the former Kent Champion.

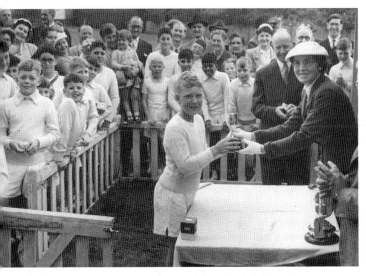

Winning at an early age. Proud Mum top left hand corner.
Normandale School, Bexhill.

Final of the Banbury Cup, playing for Brighton.

Captain of the Kent squash team.

The last time as Captain of the England Veterans Team 1992.

*Mike received his prize for winning the 0-45
British Closed Championship, from Jonah Barrington.*

*Trying to cure his morning headache with a cup
of coffee in Corisca. September 1992.*

September 24th 1993

*Blowing out the candles of his 50th. Birthday cake,
the birthday that no-one ever thought he would see.*

I was very worried about the logistics of the following morning. I wanted to travel with Mike in the ambulance, so what could I do with my car? I would have to use public transport to the hospital and leave the car at home. I had heard there was some kind of strike scheduled for the following day, which complicated matters even more. I pondered on it and decided on a plan which involved leaving home before seven and using a combination of my car, taxis and public transport. It was far from ideal, but it would probably work.

I rang my neighbour, Ros, when I came home because I did not want her to worry if I did not return for a while, or if she heard me leave early the next morning. I had left my overnight bag with Mike so that if the opportunity arose for me to stay at the new hospital at least I would have the bare essentials.

I was about to go to bed when the telephone rang. This always set my heart racing. It was not as I feared, but our friend Mary. She knew that Mike was moving hospitals and had heard about the strike. I explained my plan and her reply was to say that her husband would come straight round to collect me and would drive me up from their house the following morning. This was a wonderful solution to all my problems. It did leave me with one small but insoluble dilemma - what to do about my neighbour? It was far too late to ring her. If I put a note through her door it would wake her bull mastiff dog who would then bark and wake everyone. There was nothing I could do. Apparently she woke at 7.30am and saw my car still in the lay-bye outside our house. She rang me assuming I had overslept. When she got no reply she was really worried, came round still in her dressing gown and let herself in. She found an empty house and was very puzzled. Luckily I was able to ring her that evening to explain.

Back at Mary's house, her husband Alan was so concerned that the rest of the world would have taken to the roads that he woke me at six and we were at the hospital by the time Ros woke! This was perfect, I could help them wash and prepare Mike for his departure and also go with him for a scan which they had decided to do before he left.

Predictably, the ambulance was late. When it did arrive it had two painfully chirpy drivers who seemed to have no understanding of Mike's condition or level of confusion. This led to some fairly bizarre conversations on the journey. I gave up trying to explain and sat back and left them to it. We pulled into the new hospital; it was incredibly smart and very far removed from the Victorian pile we had just left behind. The car park was full of Rolls Royce's and chauffeurs and there was a steady stream of Arab ladies walking in. I felt that there was a very glitzy gloom about the whole place and I did not like it.

I knew we had private medical insurance, but it was hard to believe that it would cover this lot, but that was the least of my worries. Mike was being his usual co-operative self, he declined their offer of being carried out and said that he would walk. I looked aghast and protested, but was ignored. He then stood himself up and keeled over towards the window of the ambulance; my main concern was for the well-being of his head so I reached over and protected it. One ambulance driver took his whole and not insignificant weight as he leant forward and grabbed him. We all ended up in a tangled heap. Mike was uninjured but I suspect from the pained look of the ambulance driver and his subsequent limp that he had not been so lucky - he should have listened to me!

Chapter 6

OUR NEXT ABODE

We sorted ourselves out, Mike was put into a wheelchair and we went up in a lift to the top floor. It was like a five star hotel. Mike had his own room and bathroom, huge television with about twenty channels but, to my enormous concern, no visual link with the nurses. This seemed like a formula for disaster. Three minutes on his own and Mike would be climbing out of bed, over the cot sides and onto the floor. The bed was high and the floor was hard. I felt sick with worry. The nurse came in and went through all the admission formalities whilst I worried myself into an awful state. All the glitz in the world would not protect Mike if he was on his own. She was very understanding and actually suggested that I stayed, at least for the first night, to help Mike to settle in. Apparently, there was some arrangement whereby relatives can pay for the use of a 'Z' bed in the patient's room. She did say that the fee was sometimes waived if it was deemed necessary. Necessary, it was absolutely essential! In fairness, I never did pay for my bed which, when it was wheeled in, turned out to be a large and comfortable portable one which could be folded up and stored in the corner during the day. She then went out and left us to adjust to our new surroundings. The first problem was the button to call the nurses; Mike never understood the purpose of this, for the whole of his stay he would try to alter the television with it! The nurses were remarkably tolerant of being called in because he wanted the television louder or a different channel and I had not stopped him in time.

The catering staff, complete with bow ties, came in with the menu. It would have put any restaurant we had ever eaten in to shame. Mike was going to eat like a Lord, I was going to have to order on his behalf and hope to grab some bits before he devoured the lot.

I then sat back and surveyed our new environment; it was faultlessly decorated and clean, so far removed from the last place and yet I felt homesick for its shabby sense of security.

I then sneaked a look at his notes. Next of Kin:- (girlfriend) Mrs Brenda Robinson; Relationship:- Unknown. What a cheek, but it did make me smile.

There was one good thing about the location of the hospital; my mother's oldest friend, who is also my godmother, lived just around the corner. This helped enormously. I felt much less alone and telephoned her that day to make contact. She was so close that you could just see the roof of her flat from the hospital window and I now had somewhere to go if ever I needed it - what a relief.

Everything was so different; rather than being in the hustle and bustle of a ward, we were in our own little room with just one nurse on each shift allocated to Mike's care. This could mean that we would go many hours and see no-one. They liked the door to be kept closed, thus increasing the sensation of isolation, I often 'forgot' this.

That night I realised that the very best part of our new 'home' was not having to say goodnight to Mike every evening. I assembled my little bed next to his and settled down for the night. With the door closed, Mike was my responsibility and I became like the mother of a small child. With every little noise I would instantly awake, ready to do whatever he needed before he started to negotiate the cot sides en-route for the floor.

The next day things started to happen. First of all, breakfast arrived - what a feast. The waitress hardly batted an eyelid when my head popped up as well when she came in, she just went off and brought back a second cup. At least I could have some coffee. If I was quick enough I might even grab a piece of toast as well. So far so good. Then our nurse for the day introduced herself. She was a state enrolled nurse who became one of Mike's regular nurses over the next few weeks. She immediately showed concern about Mike's 'tummy bug' - the first person to show any interest at all. She took some tests and sent them off. Then the consultant radiotherapist arrived. Gone were the days of ward rounds and retinue of other doctors and nurses, this was one-to-one stuff, what a difference! He always addressed the conversation and questions to Mike out of courtesy, luckily I was always there as well as some of Mike's answers were a little unusual!

The plan of campaign was explained to us. There would be a few days of planning before the treatment would actually start. A mask would be made to cover Mike's face during treatment. This sounded quite horrendous and I wondered how he would cope as he has always tended to be claustrophobic and this sounded like the ultimate in terror, especially whilst it was being made. Then there would be a lot of high-tech planning and mathematics with the aid of a scanner to make sure that the right dose was given to exactly the right spot. I liked to hear that everything was to be so precise, but I wanted them to get on with it as quickly as possible. Once the treatment started it would be every weekday for six weeks, so we were going to get to know the hospital very well.

The consultant left and I talked about it with Mike, but he really had no idea of what was happening at all. His conversation would be perfectly lucid, but bear little relation to reality. The car park outside the hospital was cobbled and we could hear the sound of cars coming and going over the cobbles. Mike was convinced that it was a stables somewhere in Kent and he became quite cross with me when I disagreed. I think that, because of the style of the ward, he thought that it was a hotel room. I stuck all his get-well cards up on the wall in front of him so that he could see them - he liked that and the staff were most amused by their volume.

Our next visitor was the physiotherapist; I think she had been warned about what had happened before and she already knew that I was a physiotherapist myself. I really liked her, Mike didn't! She explained that they had a special gym for the patients with neurological problems and if I was in agreement Mike could have treatment twice a day and also see an occupational therapist as well. This sounded an excellent plan and we could always stop if we were unhappy. It could also help to pass Mike's days and perhaps give me the odd half hour to nip out and see my godmother or do some shopping. The first treatment was scheduled for that afternoon.

I wheeled Mike down to the physiotherapy department as planned and decided that I would stay, for the first time anyway. I had been standing Mike myself which was quite hard work for me as he still had little or no power in his left side and absolutely no balance at all. They had a standing frame, not the most modern one that I had seen, but perfectly adequate. They strapped him in so that he was vertical, with a tray in front of him and huge straps around his hips to hold him in a good position. I knew that this was exactly what he needed but it upset me dreadfully to see him tied up like this. He coped very well and would joke with the staff as only Mike can. I felt sorry for the physiotherapists - there is nothing worse than being watched by another physio, but in fact they all had specialist neurological training, which I definitely had not.

The days were starting to take shape:- Occupational Therapy from 9-10, Physio from 10-11, lunch about 1.00, then more physio from 4.00 - 5.00. This allowed Mike to have a rest after lunch and see any visitors.

The next day they started to make the mask. This involved making a plaster cast with Mike just breathing through a tube. I would have absolutely hated it, but he was as good as gold and totally co-operative. I wondered what he thought they were doing it for?

I decided to leave Mike alone with the physios that afternoon and go to see my godmother, Barbara. It was wonderful just to get out of the hot hospital atmosphere, breathe some fresh air and talk to someone in the outside world. I made sure that I was back in time to 'porter' Mike back to his room myself. I hated to think of what might happen if he was left alone in his room. They had stood him in the frame again and he was trying, not very successfully, to use his left hand on the tray.

Visitors started to arrive that day - word had got around. It was so refreshing for me to see people from the outside and

Mike loved it. He would sit in his chair and 'hold court' or sometimes sleep through an entire visit!

The results of Mike's tests came back - panic! He had salmonella. Suddenly we were thoroughly unclean and a heap of gowns and masks were outside for everyone to put on if they came in. Talk about shutting the stable door after the horse had bolted! Mike was now free of any symptoms and did anyone honestly think that I was going to sit by his bed all day wearing that lot? No chance! I had been scrupulously washing my hands all the time and I would continue to do so, but I flatly refused to gown up, especially as the problem was now over. A very officious man from the Communicable Diseases Unit came in (gowned up so much that only his eyes showed) and stood as far away from us both as he could get and asked what Mike might have eaten to give him the infection. No, I had not brought in chicken sandwiches from outside, all that had come in was the usual chocolates and fruit and his birthday cake. He seemed to think that could not be to blame. By the time he left I considered buying a yellow flag and flying it outside Mike's door. It seemed to be nothing short of a miracle that I had not had any problems.

They had made the face mask by the next day; a horrible thing in clear plastic. They fitted it and Mike went into a room with a scanner and they plotted exactly how they would blast the tumour. At last we were getting close to starting the treatment. I stood and watched on the screen whilst they did it. A sympathetic radiologist asked all about us both and said "How very sad". I could have thumped her, I wanted action, not sympathy. They had completed the planning by the weekend and so treatment was scheduled to start on the Monday morning at 8.30.

Our daily routine now had the addition of the radiotherapy so this meant having Mike washed, dressed and breakfasted by 8.30. I was certainly earning my free bed! I suspect that, had I not been there, Mike would have been wheeled down unwashed and in his pyjamas.

We had the weekend ahead of us. Pete and Chris visited on the Saturday and noticed a marked improvement. I decided to put them to good use and give Mike some extra practice with standing and starting to take a few steps. By the end of Mike's stay in hospital, most of his friends had been taught the basic rudiments of physiotherapy, whether they wanted to be or not!

Nick arrived that evening and I had some very trivial (but important to me) problems to sort out. The first was how to shave Mike. His rechargeable shaver had run out and I had no means of recharging it. I had never seen him wet shave and, stupid though it may sound, I had no idea how to go about it. Mike, by this stage, had 'designer stubble' and it did not suit him.

The second problem was laundry - where to do it and with what. Nick vanished off to the local supermarket and returned with all the necessary items. I had a lesson in wet shaving and we gave Mike a brilliant shave and even included a straight line at the back of his neck where he had started to regrow his hair again. This made him look as though he had an intentional skin-head haircut, rather than just being bald. I then set up a system in the bathroom of soaking the clothes in the bidet and drying them all around the bath. This made the bathroom look like a laundry and I waited for the staff to complain, but they never did.

We were well and truly settled in, Mike had survived his operation, thrombosis and salmonella and was about to start the treatment. I felt very positive.

The abundance of food was a problem. Mike still had this incredible appetite and apparently no mechanism to say that he was full. I survived on his left-overs, cheese and biscuits and green salad, neither of which he had ever liked. Visitors arrived bearing gifts which I had to hide as Mike was expanding by the day and these would not help him.

Monday morning came and they telephoned our room from radiotherapy to ask us to go down. I again refused the offer of a porter and wheeled him down myself. The department is in the bowels of the hospital but we found it eventually. They laid Mike on a bed and put the mask over his face. Everyone then had to leave him alone for the three minutes of treatment. The idea of Mike being alone for three minutes and not moving horrified me, although they would be watching him on a television monitor. Sure enough, he started to try to get off the bed after about the first minute. I screamed, they turned off all the machines and ran in calling out to him to stay still as they went. At least now they realised the problem with Mike appearing so co-operative and yet not able to remember any instructions at all. I decided that in future they could be more watchful and I would not look at the monitor; my screaming out was no help to anyone.

The days went by. The pattern was so rigid that there was very little time for anything else. I certainly never became bored. Caring for Mike and wheeling him around from department to department was actually a full time job.

Christmas was getting closer. I tried not to think about it, but it was an inevitable fact and there was nothing I could do to stop it. I went to the nearest shops whilst Mike was having some physiotherapy and bought a load of Christmas cards. The occupational therapist was helping Mike to write so I thought that signing his name on all the cards would be an added therapy. It was then that I noticed a really strange phenomenon about Mike's writing - he added letters. Michael would be Miiichaeeeel. He could not see this as wrong. All our friends that year received Christmas cards with this new signature of Mike's!

It seemed to me that we never had more than a few days without a crisis. Sure enough, Mike became unwell again and a urinary infection was diagnosed and he was put on antibiotics. When the nurses brought around his tablets there were so many that it seemed like a meal in itself. I also knew that his dose of steroids was likely to increase as the radiotherapy took effect and caused swelling in his brain around the tumour.

Despite everything there was still improvement in Mike's balance and mobility. In the physiotherapy department he would stand against the wall and see how long he could stay there. Twenty seconds was about his limit, but at least it was better than the standing frame. His left hand was starting to show signs of recovery. I tried to capitalise on this by putting food in it and trying to get him to put it in his mouth, food being the ultimate incentive!

Karen often visited at lunch time and I taught her how to hold his left hand in a way that would help it to recover. I also always encouraged visitors to sit on his left side to talk to him. This may sound cruel, but it made sure that he did not 'forget' his left side (which can sometimes happen when one side of the body is weak or paralysed). She and I were sitting with him one day when he looked at her and asked where Brenda was. Karen pointed to me and said "Over there". "No" said Mike, "not that Brenda, the other Brenda". He then became terribly agitated and nothing that we could say would convince him that I was there, I was another Brenda. He said that I looked the same but he was very worried about the other Brenda who was outside. Karen wheeled him all around the hospital to prove that the "other Brenda" was not there. This was no help, he was really upset. It was an absurd and impossible situation. We were starting to despair when another visitor arrived and he forgot all about it. I think that I now understand what was happening in his mind. I existed in his long term memory, I was there in the present, but as he had no short term memory, he was unable to link the two. I suppose that I should have been pleased that he cared so much but it was in fact an exasperating episode.

The events of that day left me completely exhausted. Our night nurse came on duty. She was an agency nurse whom I had not seen before. She just sat and talked to me whilst Mike slept. She asked me what she could do to help, after all I had done her job for her by putting Mike to bed myself. At that moment my idea of absolute heaven was to be able to soak in a hot bath and not worry about Mike, so she sat with Mike and I luxuriated - it was wonderful.

The next morning I awoke feeling refreshed and started on our daily routine. I knew that the one thing I had to do was to get to a bank, which might take longer than the time that Mike would be with the physiotherapists. I explained what I was going to do to the nursing staff, took Mike down to the physiotherapy department at the correct time and asked for a porter to bring him back up to the ward. I then rushed down the road to sort out a withdrawal facility at the nearest bank. Solvent at last. My purse had been embarrassingly empty for the past fortnight. I rushed back to the hospital and up to the ward - no Mike. This worried me because I knew that the physios would have gone to lunch. I ran down to the physiotherapy department and there was Mike, sitting all alone in a wheelchair. Anything could have happened. In his lovely way he said that he was just going to come and find me. He could not have walked, and if he had tried (which was very likely) he would have fallen flat on his face in an empty department. My faith in everyone who was caring for Mike reached an all time low. I took him back to the ward. I was furious. Everyone got upset: the ward blamed the physios, the physios blamed the porters, the porters blamed the ward. Who knows? At least he was unhurt.

That afternoon our solicitor telephoned. She had heard from our friend Stella how ill Mike was. She is also a good friend so she must have hated having to say what she knew she had to. She, as our legal advisor, recommended that I get Power of Attorney. It was good, sound and sensible advice, but I hated hearing it. I knew that she was right and I just wanted to get it over with as soon as possible. I also knew that I would have to mobilise some funds soon because I felt sure that this luxurious hospital would cost an awful lot more than we were insured for. I telephoned a friend who is a retired bank manager and he agreed to prepare all the necessary paperwork for me if I could get back home the following weekend. What to do about Mike? I had lost all faith in the staff to watch over him in the way that he needed. I thought of our friend Pete. He had offered to help if ever we needed it. It was therefore arranged that he would arrive early in the morning and stay with Mike until his afternoon physio session and then Nick would come after that until I returned. Poor Pete, he was worried sick about the responsibility, but I tried to reassure him that all he had to do was be there and call the nurses when required. He had taken rather a fancy to one of the New Zealand nurses so I hoped, for his sake, that she would be on duty.

I understand it all went quite smoothly. Mike's long term memory was unaffected so they talked at length about the old days at squash and watched sport on the television. Pete duly delivered Mike to the physios in the afternoon and went off for the evening to the squash club to calm his nerves with more than a few pints of beer. He had never done anything like that before and definitely had no wish to repeat the experience.

For my part, as I headed for home, having explained various things to the very worried Pete, I almost felt as though I was having an adventure. I had not been further than the local shops for ages and I felt as institutionalised as any patient. My world had just revolved around Mike and the hospital routine. Part of the journey involved a short shuttle between two mainline stations. A lady got in opposite me, obviously bursting to talk. She was an Australian, over on a visit and quite determined to tell me all about it. She established that we both had to change trains and were heading for the same destination. "How nice" she said, "we can travel together". Like heck. I warned her that we would have to run in order to catch our train. We both ran, only I ran faster! I am ashamed to say that I ran to the furthest carriage and I never saw her again. The train headed off towards Kent. The first oast house I saw made me realise how much I loved my adopted county.

It was good to be out of London and back home, if only for the day.

I did all that was necessary and was back at the hospital on time and I found Nick giving Mike his evening meal. There was some concern because Mike's leg was more swollen again.

The next morning Mike woke and complained of chest pain. He was very specific about where it hurt. I tried to convince myself that he had just pulled a muscle, but deep down I knew that the most likely explanation was that part of the blood clot in his leg had moved to his lung, a pulmonary embolus in medical terminology. This unfortunately confirmed, in my mind, that the small dose of anticoagulant he was then receiving was safe for his head but not much good for his blood clot. Common sense told me that it was obviously only a small embolus, otherwise he would not still be here. A doctor was called and he stood at the end of the bed, never came near Mike, never listened to his chest or anything. He diagnosed a pulled muscle by remote control. I was unimpressed.

The radiotherapy must have been doing something because in some ways Mike was getting worse. Night times were awful. I had to record all fluids in and out and also make sure that I always reached Mike before he attempted to get out of bed on his own. That night I made sixteen entries on the fluid chart, a rather broken night's sleep!

Chapter 7

THE RUN-UP TO CHRISTMAS

I went back to the shops the next day - they were full of Christmas decorations and very festive. I then decided that, come what may, I was taking Mike home for Christmas. I felt sure that I could cope, and knowing how much he loves his home, I felt that it could only do him good. I started to look forward to Christmas from that moment on. The consultant radiotherapist was very supportive and agreed to my suggestion. The nurses thought I was quite crazy, but were very helpful nonetheless.

That night I realised that I had to get some sleep so I decided that if I was actually in bed with Mike, holding on to him, I would sleep better knowing that I would wake as soon as he did. Two people in a hospital bed with cot sides up is not to be recommended for comfort. We had just got settled when the door opened and a new nurse whom I had not seen before looked in. "Oh, sorry" she said as she backed out - that really made me laugh! Apparently the story of the two of us in the bed is a joke that has been told many times since in the nurses office.

The nurses were beginning to realise that all was not as peaceful as it seemed behind our closed door at night and the bags under my eyes were dreadful. They suggested that I had a night at home. I explained that I was terrified to leave him. They then said that if they arranged a special nurse, just for him, would I then go? Of course, that sounded perfectly safe. I settled Mike for the night, went home and slept the clock round.

I arrived back mid-morning to a very sheepish nurse. The night nurse had left Mike for about five minutes and he had climbed out of bed and was found hanging by his arm. The doctor had been called but luckily Mike appeared to be unharmed. They now understood what I meant when I said that he could not be left alone for an instant. Because I had coped alone behind closed doors, no-one realised the extent of the problem until now. Having realised, and also because they felt so guilty, they told me they had already booked a nurse for the next night and they suggested that I stay with my godmother just around the corner. They promised me faithfully that there would be no repetition of the previous night's occurrence.

Someone must also have taken notice of Mike's chest pains because suddenly a chest Xray was ordered and, what a surprise, he had a pulmonary embolus exactly where he had said the pain was. We still seemed to have a crisis nearly every other day.

It was a fine December day and I had managed to purloin a wheelchair on a regular basis, so I decided to try taking Mike outside for a while. Now, as a physiotherapist, I should be well used to using wheelchairs but only for short distances around hospitals which are designed for them. Outside, with kerbs and other obstacles to negotiate, it was completely different. It gave me a profound respect for anyone who has to cope with a wheelchair on a regular basis. I wrapped Mike up well against the cold and off we went. For our first outing I decided to settle for just around the block. The first kerb very nearly saw Mike tipped out, but luckily he hung on with his right hand. I apologised profusely and he offered to wheel me! He still had no comprehension of why he was in a wheelchair in the first place - he could walk, couldn't he?

The last part of the walk was along some mews behind the hospital - cobbles! I had not thought about cobbles. We battled across them with Mike's bobble hat bobbing furiously as we zigzagged along. I had learnt one lesson, never try to negotiate cobbles with a wheelchair!

I was not going to be beaten by this thing. I had seen old ladies out wheeling their husbands and they coped, so would I. The next day we had finished the Christmas cards and they needed posting. We set off again. The post-box was one side of the road and we were the other, with a six inch kerb between us. It would have taken only a moment for me to cross the road and pop the letters in, but I did not dare to leave Mike unattended for that moment. We had to go on for another half mile until the kerb was low enough and even then I had to accept some help from a very unlikely couple of lads who came to our rescue.

All this exercise had given me an appetite that my daily rations of cheese and biscuits and green salad was not going to satisfy. Pete visited that night and we left the nurses in charge for the time that it took for us to eat one course in a nearby Italian restaurant. I was really tucking in until I saw a cockroach on the floor! Hence, only one course.

It was by now common knowledge that we would be home over the Christmas period and all our wonderful friends were rallying round to help. It was arranged that Chris and Heather would transport us both ways, two other friends arranged between themselves to do the shopping, another let herself into our house and cleaned it from top to bottom, and someone else offered us a turkey, stuffed and ready, together with a Christmas pudding. It was all starting to take shape.

My mother, who until now had felt very unable to be of help, was to stay with us for the whole time.

We had had two whole days without a crisis. I should have known that it was too good to last. Mike's doctor arrived, looking most concerned, and asked if Mike was a heavy drinker. I told him how much Mike drank - not a lot by any standards - and his face fell. He was hoping that I would say that Mike did drink a lot as this would have explained the abnormal liver function tests that had shown up in a recent blood test. They had no idea why Mike's liver should be playing up, so a scan was arranged with a specialist in liver problems. He was from another London hospital and was coming over to perform the test around lunch-time the following day. Mike had to be starved and the nurses put 'nil by mouth' on Mike's door and, with them agreeing to watch him, it seemed a perfect opportunity to go and have lunch with my godmother as Mike would not need any help with food and was dozing peacefully in his chair. I promised to be back in time to wheel him down to the Xray department for the ultrasound scan. I was gone about an hour and back in plenty of time. Mike's door was closed. I had learnt that this was always an ominous sign. I opened it and there was Mike, sitting in his chair with a table in front of him, sublimely happy and surrounded by the remains of a very large lunch. He had even managed to eat a grapefruit one handed. There was not a morsel left, just quite a lot of debris. He had even eaten 'my' cheese and biscuits which would have required a lot of ingenuity to open the little containers of cheese, but he had managed!

The nurses were mortified, they had failed yet again. The doctor had to be telephoned and the scan re-scheduled for the following day. There was no way that I was letting the same thing happen again. I pinned little notices to his jumper and wheelchair saying 'nil by mouth' just in case he should be out of my sight and offered some food or drink, which I knew he would eagerly accept.

The test was successfully carried out and his liver appeared to be in perfect condition. The only explanation that anyone could come up with was that it was one of the drugs he was on. This was changed to an alternative and, sure enough, over the next few weeks his liver function gradually returned to normal. Another scare over.

Mike was definitely improving physically. He was now able to walk around the room with assistance and could feed himself. The visitors were flocking in and he really appeared to enjoy their visits. I was doing daily trips to the shops whilst he was having his physiotherapy. I was trying to buy presents for everyone in an attempt to make it seem as near normal a Christmas as could be possible.

The night times were still pretty bad and starting to take their toll on me again. A friend of ours came up, unexpectedly, from Brighton and the nurses spoke to her before I did and said that I needed a break, and they would organise a 'special' nurse for Mike again if she could persuade me to be gone by late afternoon. Poor Yvonne, that had certainly not been on her agenda when she had come up, but being a kind soul she drove me home, decorated our Christmas tree and cooked my dinner. She then had another long journey back to Brighton. I felt guilty, but terribly grateful. Refreshed by a good night's sleep I went back to the hospital the following morning.

The house was nearly ready for Mike's temporary return. I was very worried about our front path and stairs as Mike was not ready to negotiate them yet. Jill came to visit the following day and she and I just walked him up and down stairs until we were more confident. He thought me a dreadful bully.

The nurses were still gently trying to persuade us not to go home. They were very worried that we would not be able to cope and they promised us a lovely Christmas if we stayed. No chance - we were going home!

One problem was the regular injections of anticoagulant that Mike needed in his stomach. Physiotherapists do not learn to give injections but I practised on an orange and was soon able to inject the fruit without difficulty (I had yet to try on Mike!).

Chapter 8

THE FESTIVE SEASON

Christmas Eve arrived. Mike had his radiotherapy really early and then Chris and Heather arrived in their car. We managed to get Mike into the front and we made the journey with no problems. My mother was waiting for us at our house, plus three huge bouquets of flowers and a basket of fruit from squash club and friends. What a lovely welcome. One important item was missing - the wheelchair that I had ordered had not yet arrived and Mike had never walked the distance from the car to our front door. Chris looked very worried but I decided that if we positioned chairs at intervals en-route he could do it in short bursts. We had no choice, we couldn't leave Mike in the car and he was certainly too heavy to carry. Mike was brilliant, he understood the need to make a supreme effort and he did. He actually did it with just one stop. Great sighs of relief all round. Mike sat down in our living room with such a look of contentment, as if he had never left. That look made it all worthwhile. My mother was with him so Chris and I started to unload the car. Mike spotted the fruit bowl and asked for a banana. He downed it in one and handed my mother the skin, ever generous! She was not fully aware of what he was like so she went out to the kitchen to put it in the bin. At that moment Mike spotted a pile of post on the table and decided to stand up and get it. My poor mother returned only a second later to find Mike on the floor. Chris and I came in to find her in an awful state, feeling that she had failed in her responsibility and let us down. No problem. I was used to Mike's ways and he was unhurt. She had learnt a valuable lesson for Christmas - never take your eyes off Mike!

Our bedroom is upstairs so it seemed sensible to get Mike up there whilst Chris was still around to help if needed. Mike again made a superhuman effort and made it up our very steep and awkward stairs with no problems. I decided that he could stay upstairs for at least two days. Our house has a spare bedroom with a convertible sofa in it, and with a bit of furniture removal, this became our living room for Christmas day. Hence, I did not have to worry about getting Mike up and down stairs.

What a strange Christmas day it was. We were joined by Karen and her boyfriend, Stephen. Mike sat in his grandfather's high backed chair with a picnic table in front of him. This was multi-purpose; he could eat off it, put things on it and it also made it extremely difficult for him to get out. We did all the normal Christmassy things. Presents were exchanged and masses of food eaten. Karen and I were exhausted running up and down stairs carrying the Christmas dinner, which was then eaten off our laps in what was normally a spare bedroom. I was just so happy to have Mike back in his home. Karen and Stephen left fairly early and I was able to get a happily exhausted Mike into bed. My mother and I could then sit just across the landing in order to watch him, and it was then that I allowed myself a drink. What nectar.

Tradition decrees that we are usually joined by my two sons, Nick and Chris, and my friend Jill on Boxing Day. I decided that with two strong young men and a doctor in the house I would risk getting Mike downstairs for the day. Somehow we would get him back up again! This was most successful. We played games, ate, drank and Mike appeared to be enjoying it all. He never asked any questions. I suppose he never remembered being away.

I brought Mike back downstairs again the next day. I was so full of confidence. Friends just flocked in all day to see him. They were all bearing gifts - mostly food, drink and chocolates. This abundance of goodies was sheer heaven to Mike. I tried to remove some of them before he spotted them, not for good, just until another day. He was becoming so excited about all the food that was arriving that he ceased to discriminate. At one stage he gobbled up two mince pies and he has never liked mince pies. He then spotted a packet of pink tissues on his table; I just stopped him in time before a handful of them were swallowed as well! I suspect that he had this voracious appetite and no sensation of taste.

A lot of the people who called in that day had only a vague idea of what was wrong with Mike. It came as a great shock to many of them, and some found it very hard to handle. One young lad who used to play squash regularly with Mike just managed to hand over a large bar of chocolate to him before dashing out to the kitchen, flinging his arms around me and sobbing. Others just sat and looked thoroughly uncomfortable, not knowing what to say. Mike, on the other hand, had a lovely day. He recognised everyone and chatted away in between mouthfuls of chocolate!

I decided that I would take him upstairs whilst there was still a strong man in the house to help if necessary. We walked to the door and around the corner, Mike then stopped dead, reached past me and grabbed a bowl of peanuts he had not spotted before.

Once we were safely upstairs and alone again Mike looked at me and said "I've had a lovely day". This was so wonderful it made all the preparations for Christmas worthwhile. It also demonstrated that Mike's memory span was now longer than the thirty seconds that it had been before. He was even able to list the people who he had seen during the day.

I suppose this was too good to last. The next day Mike started to itch all over, especially around the areas where I had been giving him his injections. I had to call our doctor because I did not know whether I should continue with the injections. He did not know either, but as we were going to be back at the hospital the following day, they could sort it out. He was not too concerned about the rash and he was very pleased to see Mike for the first time since he had arranged to have him admitted. He said that he was far better than he was expecting.

Chris and Heather took us back to the hospital the next day as arranged. The nurses were most relieved to see us. Apparently, no-one had expected us to stay the course and Mike's consultant had rung in every day to see if we were back.

We had three full days at the hospital before coming back home for the New Year. Mike was very spotty and seemed less well. They had changed his injections, so hopefully, that problem would be resolved but he was starting to hiccup again and his balance was not quite as good. His consultant wanted him to have another scan but the hiccups made that impossible. In an attempt to stop them he was given a very powerful sedative; all this did was to make him sleep all day, still hiccuping! I was to let the staff know the moment he stopped and he would be whisked down to the scanner. This happened, Mike was wheeled down and then, as he was lifted off the trolley, he started again. They decided to leave it until after the new year. I did not know how much the drugs were responsible for the deterioration in Mike and

I did so want to take him home for the new year as he had been so happy over Christmas. The day before we were due to go Mike complained of pain in his groin. There was nothing to see or feel and it appeared to pass off. Nobody seemed too concerned about it.

It was definitely more of a struggle getting Mike into Chris's car for the journey home. I just hoped that he would perk up once we got there. I was still trying to continue with the physiotherapy at home and I wrapped him up warmly and helped him to walk up and down the front path the next day. Typical Mike made a supreme effort and even asked to go further than I suggested. Then he started to shiver violently. I brought him in, wrapped him in blankets and gave him a hot drink, all the while blaming myself for allowing him to get cold. People again visited in their droves over the new year, but the ones who had been over Christmas were very worried because they noticed the deterioration. On the second day Karen visited with her boyfriend and I asked him to help me get Mike upstairs to bed. It was extremely difficult. Mike seemed unable to lift his left leg, it was so heavy. They left and I went to undress Mike. I was absolutely horrified - his leg was huge and was straining at the seams of his trousers. It was so swollen that you could hardly see where the knee was. No wonder the poor chap had found it hard to lift it - it must have weighed a ton!

I felt cold with fear. The only possible explanation was another deep vein thrombosis, only higher up in the groin this time, and even more life threatening. Here I was at home with him, with just my mother for support. I hardly dared move him for fear of dislodging the blood clot. I settled for the bare minimum of preparation for bed and he was almost immediately asleep, hiccuping again.

I went downstairs and told my mother. She, poor soul, was dreadfully worried. I asked her to sit with Mike whilst I tried to make contact with his doctor at the hospital. It seemed to take forever but eventually he rang back from his home. His advice was to give Mike a double injection of his anticoagulants and take him back to the hospital the next day. He sounded very concerned. He could also hear Mike hiccuping in the background, which was always a bad sign. Mike now seemed so ill with such a terrifying complication that I really thought he might not make it through the night. A few panic stricken phone calls later and it was arranged that Chris and Heather would drive us back the next morning, as early as possible. Goodness knows how much this disrupted their New Year's Eve celebrations, but they would not take 'no' for an answer. Jill then got into her car, complete with her doctor's black bag and drove through the fog from Brighton to be with us for the night. My poor mother, who seemed completely numb through all of this, then learned that she was about to share her bedroom for the night with Jill.

It gave me so much confidence just having Jill in the house that night. In all honesty, if the blood clot had moved, there probably would not have been anything she could have done for Mike, but this was unthinkable.

When Jill arrived she confirmed the diagnosis, gave Mike his injections much more skilfully than I could have done and we all went to bed. Mike was already asleep and I cuddled up to him. He was still hiccuping and also breathing most strangely, first a deep breath, nothing for what seemed like an eternity, then a huge deep breath. We left all the doors open between the bedrooms and, amazingly, I went to sleep. Jill and my mother lay awake all night, each one afraid of moving for fear of waking the other. As they said later, if only they had known that the other was awake at least they could have talked and had a cup of tea.

I was woken in the morning by Jill tickling my toes and saying that if we didn't get up soon we would be late. Mike had stopped hiccuping, was breathing normally and seemed much better. Totally unconcerned about all the events of the previous night and surprise, surprise, hungry!

We were all, apart from Mike, very tense on the return journey. All wondering, but not saying, what we would do if anything happened on the way. We made it - safety at last. Poor Chris was so relieved that he ate his way through about half a dozen mince pies that we had brought with us. I suspect he had been too worried for breakfast. The doctor came immediately and put Mike on a stronger anticoagulant. By the following day Mike's leg was a lot less swollen. It seemed that he had survived yet another crisis. How many lives was that now? I did feel as though he was getting through his nine lives at an alarming rate, and he was not even a cat............

I had decided not to ring Karen the previous night; she had had enough frights. She was just told that we had returned to the hospital one day early. She tried to ring us but because the whole thing had been rather hasty the switchboard had no record of Mike being in the hospital at all. She tried ringing his old room but just got a stranger. For several hours she felt as though she had lost her father. Little did she realise how close she had been to losing him altogether.

Chapter 9

THE START OF THE NEW YEAR

I was relieved to be back in the hospital but desperately worried about Mike; he had seemed quite bright that morning but then deteriorated rapidly, both mentally and physically.

The next morning I spoke to the physiotherapist and told her about Mike's thrombosis in his groin and his general state of health. She suggested that I take him down nevertheless. It was pathetic. Mike just lolled in his wheelchair, no spark of life in his eyes. She sat him at a table to just exercise his arm and he rested his head on the table and closed his eyes. All the happiness and hope that had been there over Christmas vanished. He was desperately ill again and it did not seem to relate to the thrombosis but more to the goings-on inside his head.

All the medical staff were worried as well. Mike was about two thirds of the way through his course of radiotherapy and something should have been happening by now. They arranged for a scan that lunch time in the hope that there would be a lull in the hiccups. My feeling was that, because Mike was so sick, if there was no sign of the tumour shrinking by this stage, or, horror of horrors, if it was larger, the kindest thing to do would be to stop the treatment.

The porters arrived with a trolley and at the same moment Pete came to visit, together with two friends of ours from Geneva. This was totally unexpected and I leant over Mike as he was wheeled out and said "Mike, have you seen who's here, it's Mike and Marie France". A rather petulant reply came back from the trolley. "I'm not bloody daft you know". That rendered me speechless.

Our three friends stayed with me for a while; I needed the support. Mike returned, fast asleep, after they had left I just sat quietly with him, fearing the worst. Suddenly the door opened and the 'in-house' consultant appeared. He was not Mike's doctor but had always shown an interest and been available if needed. He was grinning from ear to ear. That said it all. The tumour had shrunk far, far more than they had dared hope and the problem was again swelling inside the brain. They increased Mike's dose of steroids to combat the problem and sure enough they had an almost immediate effect. Mike seemed much more 'with it' by the following day. In memory terms he was still a long time back and became convinced that he was in a hotel bedroom and his two children were just toddlers and in the next room. He kept insisting that I went in to check that they were alright. I could cope with this. If he had asked to go in himself, the lady in the next door room might have had a bit of a surprise, but luckily he didn't.

The dramas of the previous day had obviously become distorted by the 'Chinese Whisper' effect and that night our friend Mary had a telephone call from one of Mike's friends at a Squash Club in London to say that he had heard that Mike had died and he was checking whether it was true. Poor Mary, she rang the hospital and was told that all was well, relatively speaking anyway. She then rang me to warn me in case I started to receive letters of condolence which would have been extremely upsetting. After that, she telephoned the squash club concerned to stop the rumour.

Mike was well enough to go to the physiotherapy department again the next morning and I asked for the porters to bring him back so that I could just pop around the corner to see my godmother for the first time since Christmas. I was only going to stay a few minutes but I arranged the porter just in case I should be delayed. I felt reasonably confident that the nurse, whom I had warned, would be on the alert after all the disasters of the past.

I returned to find Mike's door closed. Surely not again? I opened it and all I could see was an empty wheelchair and two feet on the floor the other side of the bed. Mike was lying on the floor between the bed and the bathroom. I bent over him, he seemed OK but I didn't want to lift him up in case he wasn't so I rang for the nurse. I was furious and very upset. Mike said that he had wanted to pack, so he had made his way around to the wardrobe and had then fallen over - he couldn't think why! It said a lot for his tenacity that he had made it that far and it was nothing short of a miracle that he had avoided banging his head as he had fallen. It did not, however, say anything for the vigilance of the nurses - yet again. They were distraught when they came in. The nurse in charge said "We've failed you again, Brenda". Too right. How could I ever leave him in anyone else's care again?

The next day I nearly had a disaster with Mike myself. I was wheeling him down to radiotherapy in the morning and the wrong lift came. There was a strange lift system whereby only one lift went all the way to the basement and if the wrong one came first you had to go in, press for another floor and send it away before you could call for the right one. I did this, but unfortunately I put both feet inside the lift to do it. The door closed on me and the lift went up with me in it and Mike unattended in his wheelchair outside. It seemed an absolute eternity before I got the lift back to the floor where Mike was. The doors slowly opened and there was Mike, looking rather perplexed but still (thankfully) in his wheelchair. "I was just coming to look for you" he said.

Since the nurse at the first hospital, many weeks before, had given me a talking to and told me not to cry but to be more positive, I had tried my very best to do just that. Some of our friends thought that I was very hard and, unbeknown to me, the nurses had become concerned about my apparent lack of emotion. One of them, a very young girl, took it upon herself, probably with all the right intentions, to come in and talk to me and explain just how serious the situation was and told me that I needed to cry. I obliged instantly of course, but at the same time I was furious with her. I felt sure that the first advice was correct and with me following that advice Mike and I were coping and, hopefully, beginning to win our battle. I did not need her to rock the boat.

Mike was starting to make slow but steady progress with his walking again. He could go further with less help. His balance was still pretty precarious and he could only stand on his own against the wall for about a minute, but this was still a vast improvement in only a few days. I now realise that his memory was on its way back in that we had another episode of "The Two Brenda's". I was alone in the room with him at the time and completely unable to cope with his frenzied anxiety about me. He was stronger this time and desperately trying to get out of his wheelchair to go and look for me. I rang for assistance and a really good nurse who had come to know us both very well came in. She sat down, ordered coffee for the three of us and gave Mike a good telling off. He hated that, being a person who always wants to please, and so he apologised for causing trouble and drank his coffee, looking less than convinced. Then he forgot all about it and peace reigned again.

The consultant radiotherapist appeared the next day and said that he had to measure the pressure inside Mike's head. This involved sticking a needle into the plastic reservoir just under the skin on top of Mike's head and reading the pressure as it came out on a gauge. He decided that I could assist him which I was more than happy to do, although watching a needle being pushed into the top of Mike's head did make me feel more than a bit odd, but I said nothing. The fluid came out and hardly moved up the gauge at all. Apparently, if there is an increase of pressure inside the brain it can move as much as a metre; in Mike's case it was barely a centimetre. What a relief. This was completely normal and it seemed as though we were having more good news than bad and fewer crises.

Every evening at about nine o'clock Mike would be given his anticonvulsant tablet. He always chewed it as though it was a sweet. That night he did the same; he munched it and then his face contorted and he said "Yuk" and spat it out. The nurse looked puzzled when I was so excited about this, but I realised that his sense of taste was finally coming back. I wanted to shout the good news to the world.

Mike's walking was improving by the day and he had just one week of radiotherapy left to go. There was no way that we were going to stay at the hospital for one night longer than necessary so we decided we should go home on the day the treatment finished, however he was. This did mean that I would have to go home for one night to get things ready. The nurses would just have to be trusted to look after him properly for once. They promised me faithfully that he would not be left alone for an instant and I believed them.

I arrived home to an answering machine loaded with messages. I played them all back and then, to my utter amazement, the last one was Mike, my old Mike. It was just the sort of message he used to leave:- "I hope you got home alright, see you tomorrow. I love you". I played it over and over again. I shall never know who's idea it was to ring me, whether he had had any help from the nurse or not, but it didn't matter, this was my Mike and he was getting better. If it was the nurse's inspiration she will never know what happiness it gave me.

I felt so happy that night; I got the house all ready for our return, made an appointment for Mike with our doctor for his regular anticoagulant blood test and then had a wonderful night's sleep.

I was still unsure about what the future held. I had no idea how much of a recovery Mike would make or how I would manage to leave him unattended in order to start working again, but that was the least of my worries, my locum could carry on as long as necessary. We were both coming home, for good this time.

Pete visited the following day. He could not believe the improvement in Mike who was now starting to walk unaided, so long as there was someone nearby with a chair at the ready. I decided that, with Pete in attendance, Mike could show off his new found skill. He walked to the nurses office, stuck his head around the door and said "Hello people". They looked dumbstruck, apparently one of them asked who he was, they had never seen him like that before. Pete and I felt very emotional and there were some moist eyes in the nurses' office.

Mike could now safely be left in his chair with a table in front of him so long as the nurses were not too far away. I went to the bank the following morning and the nurses ordered him some coffee and left him to it but kept looking in; no problems at all. That evening Mike's dinner tray had plain yoghurt on it, he has never liked it without sugar so I said I would go and get some. To my surprise Mike said not to bother as he had some. His eyes twinkled and sure enough out of his tracksuit pocket came a packet of sugar. He had secreted it away that morning when he had his coffee. This was very typical of him. Many packets of sugar had gone through the washing machine in the past because I had omitted to check every pocket. This was wonderful, not only had he behaved in a very 'Mike' way, but he had actually remembered. This was progress indeed. I was able to share my joy with Nick and his girlfriend that night when they came down from Cambridge to visit. We celebrated with an Indian takeaway in Mike's room. I had a real appetite for the first time in months and Nick was going to make sure I satisfied it!

One of the problems with Mike's memory returning was that he was now able to remember from one day to the next how much he loathed his physiotherapy sessions. He kept asking me to make excuses for him not to go. I knew that he still needed treatment, but most of all, he just needed to practice his walking, and that was well within my capabilities. The following afternoon my mother came to visit and I told Mike that I would use that as an excuse for him so long as he agreed to come out for a walk with us. My mother was aghast; she thought I was being far too ambitious. I probably was but I did know that everywhere you walk in London there are black cabs passing all the time, so if we got into difficulties we could hail one of them. I wrapped Mike up warmly and we set off, my mother doubting my sanity. We went in the direction of my godmother's flat, we might at least aim for somewhere. Mike's legs were aching but he struggled on and they actually loosened as he went. We made it to her flat and rang the bell to announce our arrival. It was the first time she had seen Mike, having a horror of hospitals she had only seen me up until then. She was amazed and my poor mother was wondering how on earth we were going to get back (so was I, but I was not admitting it!). We took the lift up to her flat and sat Mike down with a cup of tea. He now tells me that that cup of tea in her flat is his first memory of his illness. We rested for an hour and then set off back in the direction of the hospital. Mike was very tired but very determined and we made it back, although it did seem rather a long way and I was beginning to feel a bit of a bully expecting him to do it. My mother was completely speechless by this stage. I am not sure if the nursing staff or physios believed me when I said what we had done, but it was well worth it and by the next day all the aches in his legs that Mike had complained of until then had gone away and his balance had improved beyond recognition.

Something had made me put one of his squash rackets and a ball in my bag when I had come back the last time. I used this as an incentive to persuade him to go to physiotherapy the next day. Even I was not going to ask the same of him two days in a row. We went down to the physiotherapy department and I put the squash racket in his hand. We threw the ball gently at him whilst he tried to balance enough to return it. He wobbled about precariously but I then realised that the best rehabilitation from now on would be squash-orientated. He did succeed in hitting the ball and enjoyed the treatment far more than ever before. He said that there now seemed to be some sense in it.

There was now just one more day left in hospital. The visitors who arrived on that day simply could not believe their eyes. They had seen Mike only a week or so before and had been very pessimistic about his future, and now here he was chatting away to them and able to walk around his room virtually unaided. He also remembered walking to my godmother's two days before; this was real memory and a vast improvement quite beyond my wildest dreams.

I now realised that what happened from now on would be remembered quite normally by Mike, whereas the previous two and half months would always be a blank. We were both so excited about going home. Gifts had been bought for all the hospital staff who had helped and put up with us during our seven week stay; our bags were packed and all of the hundred odd 'get well' cards taken down from the wall. We were now waiting for our friend Ken to arrive to take us home. We saw him pull into the car park and he telephoned us from his car phone. He was not up to date with Mike's improvement and was completely overwhelmed when the two of us just walked out to his car arm in arm. "It's my old Westers" he said, obviously quite choked.

Chapter 10

HOME AT LAST

Once back home I did feel an enormous sense of responsibility for Mike. I know that I had undertaken nearly all of his nursing care whilst he had been in hospital, but during that time and also when we had been home for Christmas there had always been someone else around. Now we were completely on our own.

Mike was so happy to be home. He remembered nothing about Christmas or New Year and in fact his only clear memory before that was about a month prior to him going into hospital in the first instance. We had even been up to London to see a show at the end of September and he had absolutely no recollection of it at all. What a waste of money that was!

We woke up on our first morning at home and it was an absolutely filthy day, windy, wet and very uninviting. Mike, who I had always thought hated walks, especially wet ones, announced that what he wanted to do more than anything was to go for a walk on Ashdown Forest. This amazed me, but working on the principal that he needed the exercise and I wanted him to be happy, I agreed. It would certainly be nice to be out in the fresh air and in the country after all those weeks in London, but I was not at all sure that Mike was really ready for the bumpy and uneven terrain of the forest. Perhaps he had remembered the ice cream van that was always parked up there, rain or shine!

Wrapped up well against the elements we arrived at the car park high in the forest. It was the sort of wind that took your breath away. Mike was still very determined and he pointed out a clump of trees on the horizon and said that we should walk around them. There is a water filled ditch around the car park with the occasional wooden walkway over it. Mike was not going to bother himself with walkways. I was holding his arm when we reached the ditch and I was totally unprepared for him to jump over it! The amazing thing was that neither of us actually landed in the ditch. After a very undignified landing on the other side we continued around the trees as planned and arrived back, soaked to the skin, at the car and ice cream van. I suspect that ours were the only two ice creams sold that day but they were most welcome.

For the first few days we just re-adapted to being back home on our own again. Mike was now able to remember instructions and very obediently never attempted to get out of his chair unaided. I only took him upstairs once a day to bed. Every day brought more improvement; it was like a miracle.

I decided that swimming would be very good exercise for Mike, but I knew that a public pool would be impossible because Mike would need help with changing. We have a friend with a small indoor pool not far from our home and he offered us the use of it. I had mentioned swimming to the physios at the hospital before we had left and they had been less than enthusiastic, warning me that Mike might sink or just go around in circles because of his weak left side.

It would have been foolhardy to go on our own for the first time, because if Mike had got into difficulties in the water I might have been unable to manage. My friend Stella and her daughter-in-law offered to come with us, which was very noble considering how much Stella hates swimming.

Mike was really raring to go; we arrived at the pool and he was out of the car in no time. He was very nearly able to walk unaided by this time, but he did tend to be a bit tottery. The rest of us were somewhat apprehensive, but not Mike. I made him wait until Stella was in the water and then I helped him down the steps intending to follow him in. He just swam off, no problems at all. Swimming has never been his strongest point - he has always done the 'doggy paddle' - and this is what he did. He just paddled off in a straight line and with no hint of sinking. The three of us looked on in amazement. It is not a large pool but we still stopped him after ten lengths, although he could easily have carried on.

We now had another therapeutic tool at our disposal. Mike enjoyed his swims and we went most days, it also gave us both an outing. He also said that the feeling of tiredness which he had most of the time improved after he had swum.

Mike's walking was improving every day. I would now just have a hand in contact, but on the whole he was safe. The hardest part for him was walking along narrow paths (he hated that) especially if there was traffic on the road.

Our first social outing was to some friends for a dinner party. Mike found it very enjoyable, but it was all rather too much and he was very tired towards the end of the evening. I realised just how tired he was when he leant across to me and asked if I had my credit card to pay. He was so exhausted that he had become slightly confused again and thought that we were in a restaurant. This worried me, but after a good night's sleep he was fine again with no ill effects.

I started to work part-time again from home. This was good for me but it gave Mike a lot of rather boring hours to kill.

He decided that he was well enough to venture out of the house on his own, not far, just to the butchers shop a couple of doors away. We became regular carnivores with him buying meat every day, but it gave him an outing and a friendly person to talk to.

Within a few more days he felt brave enough to cross the street to the rest of the shops in our village. I knew that the butcher would keep an eye on him and, living in a village, so would everyone else. His first shopping expedition to the general store really puzzled him. There was this unfamiliar coin in his change. He was too polite to return it but was quite convinced that he had been given some foreign currency. I had omitted to tell him about the new ten pence piece that had come into circulation during his illness!

These short independent walks increased his self confidence, despite the fact that his left hand was still slightly outside his control and he had sent a whole display of jams flying on one occasion. Again, being a village with everyone knowing about Mike's condition, nobody was ever cross when this sort of thing happened.

The next challenge would have to be on the squash court. I picked a time when I knew that the club would be empty and we went onto the court. Mike looked so happy just to be standing on a squash court again. I gently hit the ball to him and he returned it. The problem was that being Mike, he could never be satisfied with just hitting the ball back to me; even on that first day he was trying to hit the ball hard and hit winners. This was too much for his centre of gravity and he kept landing on the floor, to his absolute fury. Undeterred, he kept on trying and managed to return the ball thirty times in succession on our first attempt. This was quite exhausting for me - I was trying to return the ball to him because running was not yet on the agenda, but he was trying his best to put the ball as far away from me as he possibly could!

We now had three things to do to help his physical recovery: walking (which he still hated despite his request on his first day home to walk in Ashdown Forest!), swimming and squash. It may not be text book physiotherapy but it was achieving what I would have thought completely impossible a month before. I would now work part of every day and then we would do one of these things when I had finished. Mike was also starting to do little jobs around the house; he would prepare lunch and even push a vacuum cleaner!

The work on the squash court improved his balance remarkably quickly and within a month he was starting to take steps to the ball and we were able to play a game (of sorts) with me trying to be kind to him whilst he tried to thrash me. The falls became fewer, but I became aware that he had a blind spot in his vision on just one shot. He soon adjusted to this, or else it recovered, and his sight ceased to be a problem.

It had been explained to us that the radiotherapy continues to work for about three months after the last treatment, so it was arranged that Mike should have a scan then. He was absolutely dreading this, wondering if the tumour would have started to regrow. I was sure that it would have shrunk still further, his progress was so phenomenal. But then I had seen Mike at his worst while he had no recollection of this at all and so he thought he was very bad - he should have seen himself a couple of months earlier!

We went up to London for the scan in March. Despite my confidence, it was still awful watching it being done and awaiting the results. We went in to see the surgeon who had the scans up on his viewing screen. His face said it all. The tumour had started out being three centimetres across, it was now a mere one and a quarter centimetres. What was left was just the solid core in the centre and this looked decidedly 'dead'. The surgeon was also amazed by Mike's physical progress. He asked Mike to push him away using his left hand, nearly a mistake, Mike took him at his word and practically pushed him over, such was the strength of Mike's once paralysed arm.

Mike asked him about the reservoir; he hated having a piece of plastic in his head and it sometimes felt very sore. The surgeon reassured us that this was nothing to worry about.

The next doctor we saw was the radiotherapist; he was equally thrilled with his progress. This appointment was at the original hospital where Mike had had his operation. After seeing the doctor I took Mike back to the two wards he had been on. He found it a very disturbing experience. He had just one tiny 'window' of memory just before the operation, when the steroids had started to work. A few things seemed vaguely familiar but certainly none of the staff. They, on the other hand, remembered him very well. They all rushed over and hugged him. He said it was a really strange sensation to be recognised and greeted by so many nurses, none of whom he felt he knew.

We now had something tangible to celebrate: the tumour had shrunk. We booked up for a long weekend in the smartest hotel I could find, complete with swimming pool, croquet lawn and pitch and putt. It was wonderful. I taught Mike how to play croquet, which I had learnt as a child, and he thoroughly enjoyed it. We swam every day, ate the most superb food and even played pitch and putt. All this, and it was not yet three months since he had been unable to walk, and about four months since I had been told that he probably never would.

When Mike was first home he hardly ever mentioned his job, but now he was starting to show interest in it again. I started to drive him into his office for one day a week. He could then answer the telephone, potter around the office and re-establish contact with all his customers. Their loyalty and concern for him whilst he had been so ill had been very touching. Mike does business with farmers and gamekeepers. Apparently, one of his toughest gamekeeper customers had broken down in tears when he had heard of Mike's illness. Now he and all the others were delighted to be able to talk to him again.

The world of squash was also being very supportive and helpful. Two squash clubs, Maidstone and Beckenham, where Mike had been well known and had played a lot, both invited Mike over to present their prizes on their Finals Nights. This was a lovely gesture and much appreciated by both of us.

An appointment was made for Mike to see an Endocrinologist whose job it was to juggle Mike's body chemistry now that his own body was unable to do it on its own. He asked how Mike was, Mike replied that he was very well thank you, but a bit slow to the front of the court! This, from a patient who was once thought unlikely to live and certainly not to play squash!

Spring arrived and Mike was starting to look at the garden with a gleam in his eyes. He has never been the sort of gardener to bother himself with delicate little jobs like weeding or planting out, but he just loves attacking poor unsuspecting shrubs with a saw or loppers. In our front garden, just in front of my treatment room window, there was a rather overgrown buddleia. It was a sunny Monday morning and I was working. Suddenly my patient said "I think Mike is having a lovely time". There he was, tugging, sawing and generally attacking the shrub. He was obviously thoroughly enjoying himself and it was also good exercise for him, so I was very pleased to see him do it. He took all the branches he had removed around to the back garden and a few minutes later the same patient said "I think he's having a bonfire". It was like a fog, smoke was billowing over the house. Two things worried me about this: firstly, what if he lost his balance and fell into the bonfire; and what about the neighbour's washing? I rushed into the garden. He was so content, a real little pyromaniac. He confessed he had nearly fallen in once but had just stopped himself. It was nearly burnt out by this stage, so I said nothing, he was so happy. I did apologise to the neighbours who were most understanding.

The next day he cleared up all the mess and decided to turn to the compost heap. This is in the corner of the garden, backing onto where our neighbour must once have had an outside privy. There is a vicious pipe coming through the wall, a bit like the old overflow. Mike was bending down and came up quickly, right onto this pipe. He badly hurt his head. I made him sit down and looked at his head, he had not broken the skin and there was no lump, apart from the lump of the reservoir, which was worryingly close to where he had hit himself. He recovered very quickly and was soon back out in the garden again.

I felt rather like the mother of a small child. I knew I must allow him his freedom to regain his confidence but I wished that he could have slightly more of an instinct for self-preservation.

Summer was coming and we started talking about a summer holiday. Mike never feels as though he is on holiday unless we are abroad. This made me rather nervous; I was not sure I was ready to do this. The problem was solved by our friend Sue. She and her husband have a little converted fisherman's cottage on the north coast of Brittany. The cottage next door is owned by her father, a doctor with a special interest in neurology. She offered us use of the cottage at the time when her father would be there. Perfect. I went ahead with all the ferry booking and arrangements confident that if I needed any help, Sue's dad, Stanley, would be just next door.

Spring turned to summer and Mike's progress continued relatively uneventfully. He had only two main complaints: one was the soreness on his head where the reservoir was and the other was a nasty, deep-seated lower back ache which I, as a physio, was completely unable to diagnose, locate or treat. It was most odd. We did a lot of really enjoyable things, one of which was to go to the Test Match at Lords with Pete. Then we went to Chris and Heather's wedding. At all of these events I had the same feeling of wonderment that we were actually there together and leading a near normal life.

We were both looking forward to the holiday. We were to take the overnight boat from Portsmouth to St. Malo and it was only a short drive from there, so my ability to drive on the right was not going to be tested too much. We had even arranged to meet our friends Stella and David whilst we were there and spend a day on their boat. Mike was a bit quiet about that - he hates boats! Two weeks before we were due to go on holiday Mike's head became really sore and tender. We made an appointment to see our doctor on a Saturday morning. He knows that it is almost unheard of for Mike to make an appointment to see him, despite all of his illnesses, so when he saw Mike's name on the list for that morning he said he knew that we were about to "bowl him a difficult one". He was right. He had no idea why it was hurting so much but he put Mike on antibiotics just to be on the safe side. He was worried about us going away and asked to see Mike again before we left. The antibiotics improved things enormously and by the time Mike went back to see him again the pain had virtually disappeared. Big sighs of relief all round and we were given permission to go on holiday but Mike was prescribed some more antibiotics as a precaution.

The night before we were due to leave we had packed and were ready to go and Mike wanted to ring Karen. Whilst he was talking to her he called me. There was liquid running down the side of his head. I mopped him up and investigated. There was nothing to see and it stopped almost immediately. I added some disinfectant, cotton wool and dressings to our luggage just in case. I re-checked his head in the morning before we left, again there was nothing to see and Mike seemed very well and very excited about the holiday.

Chapter 11

MID-SUMMER HOLIDAY

We had booked a night crossing, but Mike was so anxious not to miss the boat that we arrived about three hours early. To think that in the past Mike had never been early for anything. In fact we were usually the last car allowed on the boat, just squeezed in before they shut the doors. Perhaps this was the personality change that I had been told to expect, if so it was probably a change for the better, but three hours was a long time to kill at a port.

It was a lovely trip. We had an excellent meal on board and we both slept well. The drive to the house was easy and we arrived mid-morning. We said hello to Sue's parents next door and started to unpack the car. It was a lovely old cottage with a large stone floored living area downstairs and two bedrooms and a bathroom upstairs. The front garden was small with a raised patio area for a table and chairs, and a wonderful view of the sea. It all boded really well for a wonderful week's holiday.

Suddenly Mike called me. Liquid was again running down his face, only this time you could see a small, deep hole about the size of a pinhead. I cleaned him up, thankful that I had packed the cotton wool and disinfectant, and then called Stanley. Poor chap, we had only just arrived and were already mucking up his holiday. He was reassuring and we covered up the little hole with a dressing - not easy when it is surrounded by hair.

All my instincts were to turn straight around and head for home. Mike was completely unable to understand this. He felt absolutely fine and as far as he was concerned he had a small sore on his head which was a lot less painful that it had been for months. He had looked forward to his holiday and nothing was going to spoil it.

I had to go along with this so we spent a lovely day exploring the area and sitting on beaches. That evening we had a meal out in a restaurant overlooking the harbour. During the meal Mike made a small, but completely irrelevant remark about a boat that we could see. I went completely cold. It was very trivial yet horribly reminiscent of his confusion of the past.

I checked the 'little hole' that night and nothing much had changed. I was really worried by now. The following morning it was leaking again and I could feel a hard rim under the skin which I had not felt before. The hole was larger and what looked like gauze could be seen. Poor Stanley had his breakfast interrupted again. This time he suggested that we use the telephone in his house to ring Mike's doctor back home. I felt a lot less remote when, with the wonders of modern dialling, I was soon through to the surgery. It was answered by one of the practise nurses whom we knew very well. I explained that I was ringing from France and that Mike had a leaking hole in his head which I could see into. "Oh my God" she said and went for the doctor. He promised to ring the surgeon and to ring us back that evening. In the meantime he suggested that we got some stronger antibiotics. He also asked me to take Mike's temperature regularly.

Mike was still thinking that this was a lot of fuss over nothing and was totally resistant to any suggestions that we should go home. I thought you could buy antibiotics over the counter in France so we walked to the local chemist. No luck, so we bought the thermometer and the chemist gave us the address of a doctor. The idea of making an appointment to see a French doctor for the prescription and trying to explain Mike's very colourful medical history in my very poor 'schoolgirl' French did not appeal. I went back to Stanley. He pulled out a tatty envelope full of tablets. Apparently he has a recurrent bone infection and always carries antibiotics with him in case it flares up again. He said they were not the best ones for Mike but would be a lot better than nothing. He really did save the day.

I spoke to our doctor that night, as arranged, and told him what we had done. He had spoken to Mike's surgeon who said it was probably just a stitch and not to worry, no need to come home. He had also had the presence of mind to get the surgeon's home telephone number which he gave to me. At least Mike was now dosed up with Stanley's antibiotics and his temperature was normal. We were planning to spend the next day on Stella and David's boat and, reassuringly, they are also both doctors. I changed the dressing on Mike's head before we left for the boat. The hole was now about half a centimetre across and there was definitely visible mesh at the bottom. The ridge around the edge was also becoming harder and I started to wonder if the reservoir was about to break through the skin.

We arrived at the boat which was moored on a pontoon in a very picturesque harbour. Mike was unimpressed but, determined as ever, he managed to climb onto the boat which even I found extremely difficult. David, being an eye surgeon, had a magnifying glass with which to look into the hole. He was extremely worried and said that what we were seeing was the plastic of the reservoir and the fluid that was leaking was cerebro-spinal fluid from inside Mike's brain. He made me promise to ring the surgeon at home that night.

I sensed their anxiety, Mike however was far more concerned by the fact that he was on a sailing boat for the first time in his life and was not at all sure that he wanted to repeat the experience.

It was a lovely day, despite Mike's head. We took their boat from it's mooring and down the estuary past a lot of very pretty villages. We then dropped anchor and enjoyed a thoroughly French lunch of cheese, meat, salad, bread, melon and, of course, wine. Mike decided that he could cope with this part of boating but when Stella and David realised that the anchor was dragging and we were just drifting with the tide, he rapidly went off it again. It was raining and squally by now so they had to don all their waterproofs before they could resolve the problem. We stayed snug and warm in the galley with Mike wondering if he was about to find out what it was like to be ship wrecked. It was, of course, no problem. The motor was started, Mike having voiced a distinct preference to motor as opposed to sail, and we made a sedate return to harbour. They were staying on the boat that night and returning to their holiday home in Southern Brittany the following day. We drove back to our cottage. Mike said he had enjoyed his first experience on a boat and was glad he had been, but he did still remain fundamentally a landlubber. I thought that, considering his poor balance and still weak left side, he had done brilliantly well to climb on and off the boat as he had.

I rang the surgeon that evening, but he was out. His wife said that he would return my call as soon as he came in. Mike went to bed and I sat beside the telephone until the early hours, but it never rang. Eventually I went up to bed and slept fitfully to be woken at about eight in the morning by the telephone. It was the surgeon and when I told him what was happening he said that he wanted us to go straight home and to take Mike to the original hospital and he would operate to remove the reservoir and all the bits of plastic tubing attached to it.

Stanley and his wife were leaving that morning and catching the eleven o'clock boat from St. Malo. I could see them loading up the car and just about to leave. I knew that it would be completely impossible for us to catch that one - Mike was still asleep in bed and we had not started to pack or clean up the house. I spent a moment or two at a loss as to what to do. I then found an old ferry brochure that I had packed, just in case. I saw that there was a boat sailing from Caen later that day. It was a lot further for me to drive but I thought we could probably catch it if we could be up, dressed, packed and ready to go in an hour. I did not fancy negotiating with the ferry company in French so I rang the telephone number in England. I was expecting a problem, but it was so easy. Our booking was immediately changed and all we had to do was get there in time and report to the booking office at the port.

It was a very rude awakening for Mike; he was hoping for another day on the beach, instead of which he had to be up, dressed and breakfasted in under the hour with the knowledge that we were going home early and he was going back into hospital for another operation. I actually felt enormously relieved that we had been told to go home. I was sure it was the right thing to do. Mike was far less convinced and terrified about the prospect of another operation.

Despite the urgency of the situation there was no way I could leave someone else's house without cleaning it. We ate our breakfast on the run. I stripped the beds and cleaned the bathroom whilst Mike swept right through the house. Our personal packing left a lot to be desired. Dirty bedlinen and towels were just thrown into the boot of the car, clothes just slung into the two suitcases and all the odds and ends went in loose. We did actually manage the whole thing in under an hour. It was probably a good thing to be so rushed - there was less time to think about things.

We had no idea of the route to Caen and Mike had to map read. The skill of route planning and reading a map, which he had learnt at school, appeared completely unaffected by his illness and he coped brilliantly. It was the furthest I had ever driven in one go (pathetic lady driver that I am) and by far the furthest I had driven on the right. Consequently, there was a certain sense of achievement when we reached Caen. This was somewhat premature as the port is actually about another fifteen kilometres from the town itself. Anyway, we did just make it in time and the ferry company were true to their word and our tickets were ready. There was the boat, waiting to take us back to England, and we were in time to catch it - what a relief.

Stanley's emergency supply of tablets were obviously still doing their stuff and Mike was still perfectly well despite the fact that I had noticed that the reservoir had actually broken through the skin and there was about half an inch of plastic sticking out of the top of Mike's head with fluid still leaking out. As we drove on board there was a photographer taking everyone's picture, this would then be displayed in the hope of a sale. We went to look at our photo; there we were, smiling cheerfully, the only evidence of our problems being a piece of white elastoplast stuck to the side of Mike's head. I decided that this was not a picture I wanted to buy!

The best way to pass the journey seemed to be in the restaurant, so we joined the queue. The lady in front looked vaguely familiar and she kept glancing at me. I felt I knew her from about ten years before when I had lived in Brighton, and after several minutes curiosity got the better of me and I introduced myself. As soon as she said her name, it all came back. I had known her and her husband quite well, albeit a good few years before. We all sat down together for our meal and it was just what we needed because it stopped us thinking too much about what was to come.

We docked at Portsmouth and I debated driving Mike straight up to the hospital, but he still seemed very well and I knew he would absolutely have hated the idea, so I drove us back home for the night. At least we were back on English soil should anything go wrong. As soon as we walked in the door the telephone rang. It was Stella. She and David had been so worried about us they had been ringing the house in France and our home all day until they got a reply.

I never realised how many people in our village subconsciously notice my car parked outside our house. Consequently, when it reappeared several days ahead of schedule, a lot of people realised that something must have gone wrong. We were utterly exhausted that evening and so the heap of debris in the boot was simply turned into a heap of debris in the hall and we went to bed.

Chapter 12

ANOTHER OPERATION

The next day we drove to the hospital, very miserably. Mike was admitted onto the ward that he had been in for the latter part of his stay in that particular hospital eight months before. Several of the nurses recognised him and he was made to feel very welcome, but this was no consolation. He was put into a small, single side ward where he just sat on the bed looking far, far more nervous than he had ever done before, probably because this time he was much more aware of what was happening. A junior doctor went through all the admissions formalities; there was one small problem in that they had no supply of one of the tablets Mike had to take regularly. I said that I always carry a supply so he could have one of them, at which point I dropped it on the floor. "Never mind" said the doctor, "it can join all the others". I laughed politely and crawled under the bed to retrieve it. He was not joking, there were three other tablets there of various shapes and sizes amongst the dustiness. A horrifying thought - what if a child visiting had crawled under the bed and picked them up? When was the ward last cleaned?

It was Karen's birthday and she came up to visit. Mike felt dreadful that this was how she was spending her birthday. The next visitor was the anaesthetist. This worried Mike because the surgeon had said that they would try to do it all under a local anaesthetic. He had obviously had second thoughts. This plunged Mike so low into his fear and depression that they prescribed him something to help him to relax.

When the surgeon did eventually come in, he said he was enormously relieved to see us. He had been very worried that it might "have just gone". I decided not to ask him to elaborate on exactly what he meant by that. He explained that because there must be an infection in Mike's head he would have to be the last one to go into the theatre that day, which meant a long wait.

Eventually Mike dropped off to sleep just before the porters came to collect him, he was so unaware of what was going on by that stage that I decided I would not follow the same route to the theatre as I had done before. It was not going to be of any help to him and would definitely have finished me off. He would have to be back in the main ward that night so they could keep an eye on him, so I busied myself moving his belongings out of the side ward. I then went off to have a coffee because even if it only took the predicted ten minutes to do, there would also be a certain amount of preparation and recovery time. I went back to the ward about half an hour after he had gone. I wondered if he might be back already, but there was still a nasty gap where his bed should be. The nurses were incredibly busy so I was reluctant to ask or make a fuss. After about three hours of patiently sitting by the empty bed space, I could bear it no longer and I went and asked the staff nurse if she could find out what was going on. She rang the recovery room by the theatre but Mike was not even there yet. No news at all. This was so horribly like history repeating itself that I just had to get out of the ward and be by myself. I knew that if Mike was not yet in the recovery room it would be a little while before he was back on the ward. I went into the chapel and just sat, and the peace in there helped to calm me down.

I returned to the ward to resume my anxious vigil. It seemed an eternity before the nurse came over to say that Mike was ready to come back to the ward. I decided that he must be alright, otherwise he would have been transferred to the high dependency ward downstairs, this ward was for the far less ill patients. I now sat beside the empty space, completely unaware of anybody or anything apart from the doors through which they would be wheeling my Mike. At last they appeared and I saw a bandaged head, then the porters misjudged the gap and the bed crashed into the door frame, the bandaged head wobbled hideously. I rushed over, nobody seemed to be even slightly concerned and Mike was still fast asleep.

I sat with him as he gradually woke up. He seemed fairly confused and kept vomiting. I was glad that I was there with him. Time was getting on and it was well into the evening by now. I wanted to stay with Mike and I certainly did not feel capable of driving home, so I just stayed put. The night staff came on duty and brought me a blanket. I construed this as tacit consent for me to stay the night in the ward. Mike drifted in and out of consciousness and kept on vomiting. Eventually he became more peaceful in the early hours of the morning. It was then that I became aware of all the noises that go on at night in a neurological, mixed, open ward. Snuffles, cries, grunts, snores, nurses moving about - how could anyone ever sleep? I also became aware of how uncomfortable I was. I was fully clothed, sitting on a hard plastic chair, with a blanket over my feet which were resting on a foot stool. I did nod off at about six in the morning, only to be woken almost immediately by a nurse tickling my toes to wake me. Mike was starting to try to get out of bed, definitely not allowed! He had looked down and seen that I was asleep and was trying to go to the toilet on his own. He seemed a lot better but was still rather confused. He did get back into bed, with a small protest. I wondered what the huge bandage was covering.

The busy routine of the ward got underway. Mike, to his disgust, had been told that he must stay in bed, so I helped him to wash, remembering where to find everything from before. I then wondered what to do about myself. A night in my clothes in a hot ward made me feel distinctly unpleasant. I decided that the best thing to do was to simply help myself to a clean towel and make use of a shower. Bliss. I was now ready to face the day and my extremely disgruntled Mike. He wanted to come home but I knew he was not well enough. He was not to be allowed out of bed that day. They moved him back into his own little side ward and arranged for a small television as a peace offering. He would not be placated. A ten minute operation he had been told - over three hours; a local anaesthetic he had expected - he had been given a general; to go home the same day he had been told - now he was about to stay a second night! He was definitely not a happy chap. I stayed all day with him doing crosswords and chatting whilst he dozed on and off. We saw the surgeon later in the day and he told us what an awful battle he had had to get all the plastic tubes out of Mike's brain. They had become well and truly stuck. It was a very good job that Mike had had the general anaesthetic in the first place because they would certainly have ended up having to give him one eventually. All this tug of war inside Mike's head would be bound to create some swelling so I now understood why he was slightly confused and a bit fractious. The huge bandage was a pressure bandage covering two small incisions and one larger one where the reservoir had been. I did feel rather sorry for the surgeon; he had been so proud of his handiwork in the first place and now he had

had to work late one evening to remove it all. There was one interesting development in that the back pain which Mike had been complaining of for all those months had completely disappeared, so already he was better off. The main risk now was an infection, meningitis, so Mike was put onto a really powerful antibiotic.

I knew that I would have to go home that night and leave him again - it was horribly reminiscent. He made me promise to return as early as possible the following morning because he was quite determined that he would be coming home. The stress and strain of all these events had taken their toll on me and I drove home, went straight to bed and overslept. This meant that I did not arrive back at the hospital until ten o'clock. I was in the dog-house. There was Mike, bag packed, coat on, just sitting on a chair beside his bed waiting to come home. The junior doctor, who looked as though he had been working non-stop for the last three days, had to come in order to prescribe the drugs for Mike to take home. He then tried to persuade the hospital pharmacist to come in on a Sunday morning to dispense them but she refused. This meant that I would have to find a chemist on our way home. I could have done without that added problem. I knew that Mike should not really be coming home yet, but he had been so insistent that they had reluctantly agreed. I would now have to leave him in the car whilst I went to a chemist. He was showing signs of confusion again so I just had to hope that he remained still. Double yellow lines were everywhere, and being a law abiding citizen, I parked a long way from the chemist so as not to break the law - very silly really as Mike's well being was much more important than a traffic regulation. I ran both ways and found Mike still there on my return, fast asleep, he did not even remember me going.

Having arrived home Mike then took to his bed for four days, totally out of character. He had obviously forced himself to get up in order to go home and now that he was back, he was just letting his body dictate to him and this was what it told him to do.

Our doctor visited every day and was most concerned, but Mike had been lying there listening to the Test Match and was always able to give him an accurate run-down of the scores, so his memory was obviously perfect. On the fifth day he was suddenly better. He just got up and was completely different, no back pain and with better balance than he had had for months. All that he had to show for it all was a small bald patch and a few stitches. Rehabilitation was resumed!

Chapter 13

THE ICING ON THE CAKE

We decided to get married in the autumn, which was very short notice for all the preparations, but we managed it. We invited all the friends who had been so wonderfully supportive throughout Mike's illness. What a wonderful day, a real dream come true. We then went to Ireland for our honeymoon.

ONE YEAR AFTER THE OPERATION

Mike was now able to apply for his driving licence to be re-issued. This all went very uneventfully and there he was, able to drive again. He was delighted that he could, and yet surprisingly nervous about it. He drove very short distances at first with me beside him. Then we realised that I was the one making him nervous so he then drove on his own and was much more confident.

Mike celebrated his fiftieth birthday. Remembering his forty-ninth (which was more than he could do!) it really did seem as if miracles do happen. We shared some champagne and the top layer of our wedding cake with a few friends.

THREE MONTHS LATER

Mike was now ready to start working full time again. He took on a horrid little red van as a company car and started his regular visits of farmers and gamekeepers as if he had never been away.

THREE YEARS ON

Mike has been invited to play squash for Brighton again. For years he had played in their first team but he was more than happy to play at the bottom end of their third team. We arrived at the club where he was to play. There would usually just be the team members, but this time a whole crowd of his old friends had come to support him. His opponent was more than somewhat puzzled by this gallery of spectators and even more amazed by the array of spectacular winning shots from Mike. Everyone cheered, and when Mike eventually won the match, the applause was fantastic. It was his love of squash and the love that other squash players have of him that had brought him through - now he was there!

Mike now plays squash several times a week; some games he wins, some he loses, but in that all important match (for his life) he won through - albeit 10-9 in the fifth.